YOUTH UNEMPLOYM

Its Psycholo

Youth Unemployment in the 1980s:

Its Psychological Effects

MICHAEL H. BANKS and PHILIP ULLAH

CROOM HELM
London and Sydney

© 1988 M.H. Banks and P. Ullah

Croom Helm Ltd, Provident House, Burrell Row,
Beckenham, Kent, BR3 1AT

Croom Helm Australia, 44-50 Waterloo Road,
North Ryde, 2113, New South Wales

British Library Cataloguing in Publication Data

Banks, Michael H.
    Youth unemployment in the 1980s: its
    psychological effects.
    1. Youth — Employment — Great Britain
    2. Unemployment — Great Britain —
    Psychological aspects
    I. Title II. Ullah, Philip
    331.3′4137941   HD6276.G72

ISBN 0-7099-3969-8

Printed and bound in Great Britain by Mackays of Chatham Ltd, Kent

CONTENTS

Acknowledgments
List of Tables

ACKNOWLEDGMENTS

At the centre of this book is a research project which was
funded by the Department of Employment, to whom thanks are
due, and especially to the Liaison Committee that provided
helpful assistance. Thanks are also due to Professor Peter
Warr, to MAS Survey Research who carried out the fieldwork,
and to Jane Hall and the late Norma Shepherd who skilfully
typed the manuscript. Not least we are grateful to the many
young people who patiently answered our questions. Needless
to say the opinions expressed here are those of the authors.

TABLES

Tables

Chapter 1

YOUTH UNEMPLOYMENT IN A HISTORICAL CONTEXT

It is important to remind ourselves that the problem of youth unemployment is not a new one, but that it has been defined in different ways according to the point in history at which it occurred. Therefore we consider it important to see youth unemployment in its historical context, which involves differing economic circumstances, societal values, public awareness and political outlook. By way of introducing this book we will briefly review the key writings on adolescence, entry to work and unemployment from the late Victorian period up to the early post-war studies, with the aim of illustrating how and why youth unemployment has been defined as a problem.

It is worth noting, first of all, that psychosocial concepts of adolescence have varied greatly over time (Aries, 1962; Kett, 1977). The term adolescence was rarely used prior to the 18th century and although the characteristics of puberty were well recognised, little psychological significance was attached to them (Rutter, 1979). The reaching of adulthood was determined largely by the acquisition of economic independence, regardless of when physiological maturity was reached. There is a convincing argument that the discovery of adolescence in the 19th century can be attributed to the middle-classes (Gillis, 1974). It was mainly the better off families who could afford to do without the work, and therefore the income, of their children. Then by the turn of the century beliefs about the vulnerability of teenagers ushered in a sequence of protective legislation that was to increasingly affect all social classes. As the figures on educational participation in Table 1.1 show, during the early part of the 20th century more and more young people were being removed from the labour market.

These wide-ranging changes in society coincided with the articulation of the image of the teenage years as tumultuous, disturbing and generally in need of adult guidance.

1

Table 1.1: Percentage of Age Groups in Full-Time Education in Great Britain, 1870-1962

Age	Year			
	1870	1902	1938	1962
10 years	40	100	100	100
14 years	2	9	38	100
17 years	1	2	4	15
19 years	1	1	2	7

Source: Marsh (1965)

Some of the earliest work on young people and the labour market, carried out during the late Victorian period, defined the problem as one of 'boy-labour'. The trends during this period, investigated by social historians such as Beveridge and Tawney, can be characterised as follows. First, there was believed to be an excess demand for juvenile labour in certain 'blind-alley' occupations. Second, juveniles were recruited straight from school and discharged from employment after two or three years, without training, to join the reserve army of unskilled labour, while their place was taken by a new generation (or cohort) of school-leavers. Third, unemployment among 14 to 17 year olds was not considered a problem; the difficulty arose in the late teens if the youngsters failed to make the transition to more secure and skilled employment. The position was well summarised by Beveridge:

> ... it is clear that a great many boys and girls on leaving school enter occupations in which they cannot hope to remain for more than a few years and in which they are not fitted for any permanent career. With the ... development of trades and processes to which apprenticeship has never been applied, there has come a break-up in the continuity of industrial life. The principle of apprenticeship was that people should enter in early youth the craft in which they would remain to the end. At the present time ... some (industries) use far more boys than they can possibly find room for as men .... They are the 'blind-alley' occupations which have to be abandoned when man's estate is reached .... (The boys) enter, not as learners, but as wage earners, doing some work too simple or too light to require the services of grown people. When, therefore, they themselves grow up and begin to expect the wages of grown people, they

must go elsewhere to obtain these wages. They leave or are dismissed and their places are taken by a fresh generation from the schools. They find themselves at eighteen or twenty without any obvious career before them, without a trade in their hands, and with no resources save unskilled labour.   They go therefore – very likely after a period of military service – to overcrowd that already crowded market.

(Beveridge, 1909, pp.125-6)

Similarly, in his study of Glasgow, R.H. Tawney describes in considerable detail the contrasting early careers of tradesmen as compared to unskilled workers, noting particularly the frequent job changing and frictional unemployment of this latter group (Tawney, 1909).

The next phase of writings included the social surveys of the pre-1914 period. Outstanding amongst these investigations was the famous Rowntree survey of York in 1910, in which, somewhat to the authors' surprise, a high level of youth unemployment was revealed. Rowntree and Lasker (1911) noted three characteristics of the young unemployed: poor educational attainment; low intelligence, physically weak or disabled, from 'unsatisfactory' homes; and previous employment in unskilled, casual labour with frequent job changing. Frequent job-changing was also the focus of a later study of 14 year old school-leavers in Birmingham (Freeman, 1914), showing clearly the deteriorating prospects (sample also interviewed at 17 years) of the chronic job changers.

Subsequently, there were the studies carried out during the Great Depression of the late 1920s and early 1930s. During this period of world recession levels of youth unemployment in Britain were very high and there was great concern about the demoralisation of young people and the possibility of political unrest.   One of the major investigations was of 21,000 school leavers in Lancashire (Jewkes and Winterbottom, 1933). This found that employment levels of 14-15 year olds was higher than those of older age groups, because industry was shedding labour at 16, due to additional financial overheads incurred. This led to the paradox that those with longer periods of education were least able to find employment. Another major study was of 18-25 year olds in Glasgow, Liverpool and Cardiff (Cameron, Lush and Meara, 1943). This found that unemployment increased with age within the sample, that the risk of unemployment was very unequal and that a past history of unemployment was a good predictor of future unemployment. Unlike Jewkes and Winterbottom, Cameron et al. found unemployment rates to be lower amongst those who left school later. Chronic unemployment (no more than six months' employment in three years) was more common amongst those who were married. Cameron et al. place great emphasis on the role of personal

3

appearance in determining employment status, noticing that the chronically unemployed were shorter, lighter and less well dressed than the others. They also noted the grievances of the young unemployed: they complained of getting only substandard jobs through the employment exchange whereas the best jobs came through personal influence; there was a high level of dissatisfaction with pay; and there was a feeling of being used as cheap labour, therefore leading to frequent job changing.

Another study corroborated these findings (Jewkes and Jewkes, 1934), and added an interesting finding in respect of geographical mobility. The authors found a higher employment success rate amongst those young people who moved with their families, within the county and across regions, to more economically prosperous areas.

Perhaps the dominant theme in unemployment research is what might be called the model of individual pathology. This may be characterised by an emphasis on the effects on individuals in terms of despair, exhaustion, deprivation, depression, apathy, and so on. Although this theme is very much alive today it can be summed up vividly with the following quote from a 1938 report:

> The depression and apathy which finally settles down in many of the homes of these long-unemployed men lies at the root of most of the problems which are connected with unemployment. It is one of the reasons why they fail to get back to work. It is one of the reasons why the majority of them 'have not the heart' for clubs or activities of other kinds, and it is one of the reasons why their homes seem so poverty stricken. 'I don't know how it is', said a young married woman in Blackburn, 'but these last few years since I've been out of the mills I don't seem able to take trouble, somehow; I've got no spirit for anything. But I didn't use to be like that.' One of us who saw her had little doubt 'how it was'. The woman looked thin and ill, and it was clear that what food there was was going to the children.
>
> (The Pilgrim Trust, 1938, pp.148-9)

Another study, this time specifically of young people, carried out during the period of the Depression, includes some vivid portrayals of the psychological effects of unemployment. The following quotations serve to illustrate the psychological deprivation uncovered during Cameron et al.'s survey of Disinherited Youth:

> From the very start of their industrial life, at fourteen, they had experienced unemployment, so that even the youngest of them at age eighteen, were personalities that had matured, during those very important and

4

impressionable four years against a background of unemployment, in some cases slight, in other cases entirely devoid of any pattern of work as a part of life.
(Cameron, Lush and Meara, 1943, p.65)

One young man described his feeling while unemployed as 'living death'. Many more may have felt this, but could not express it. Unemployment due to conditions of world trade, or technological changes in industrial organization, meant nothing to them. Such explanations left them cold. What mattered to most of them was that they were fit and able to work and wanted it badly, not so much as an end in itself as a means to an end. They needed the money, their homes needed the money, and it would be money earned by their own effort. One young wife put it thus: 'Somehow when it's money that your man has worked for it goes further.' Unemployment was a new and strange feature in the lives of a few. They were anxious and alert. They expressed their youthful impatience with the slow moving queues and hurriedly left the Employment Exchange after 'signing on'. Others, however, had acquired the art of patience. They had longer and more frequently recurring experiences of unemployment. With drooping shoulders and slouching feet they moved as a defeated and dispirited army. They gave their names, signed the necessary forms and shuffled out of the Exchange. This twice a week, was the only disciplined routine with which they had to comply.
(ibid, p.5-6)

The central problem of the lives of most of these young men is one of maintenance of self-respect. Rightly, they feel a need to take their places in society, achieving in their own right the means of living. Much of their conduct, irrational and unreasonable to outward seeming, becomes understandable if regarded in its perspective, as part of a struggle for the retention of self-respect. The attitude of many men who refuse training - a problem discussed in a later chapter - has its origin here; similarly, their resentment at being 'messed about' can be understood for what it really is -- an essay in self-respect. They have no function in society. They are the unwanted hangers-on of a community in the life of which they are unable to play their full part.
(ibid, p.80)

The wastage and personal disaster brought about by prolonged joblessness among the young has been described as one of the worst blots on the country's record between the two World Wars (Beveridge, 1944). The same author goes on to stress how the weak position of youth in the free democracies in times of peace stands in poignant contrast to what is required of them in times of war. If the plight of the unemployed needs further emphasis Beveridge once more provides it:

> The greatest evil of unemployment is not the loss of additional material wealth which we might have with full employment. There are two greater evils: first, that unemployment makes men seem useless, not wanted, without a country; second, that unemployment makes men live in fear and that from fear springs hate.
>
> (Beveridge, 1944, p.248)

The next phase included studies carried out during the decade and a half after World War II. Because of the pre-occupation at this time with extending educational opportunities and creating a full employment society, research tended to concentrate on the transition from school to work. Ferguson and Cunnison (1951) suggested that differences between those in settled and those in stop-gap employment reflected underlying differences in attitude to work. Those in stop-gap jobs changed jobs more frequently, had greater experience of unemployment, were more hostile to work, less well trained, and more prone to dismissal. Amongst the family background factors it was found that taking responsibility at home was associated more strongly with employment record than was the standard of living. Harris (1960) found job-changing to be greater among secondary modern school-leavers, but largely accounted for by a hard core of chronic job-changers. This study curiously suggested that considerable social mobility was offered by the labour market, in that only a weak correlation was found between fathers' occupations and those of the children. Baxter (1975), with data from 1952 and 1956, found that high levels of job changing and frictional unemployment were associated with dismissals for disciplinary reasons. The problem of job changing was exacerbated by the low level of unionisation, particularly in distribution trades, and poor personnel practices of small firms. Carter (1969) at a time of relatively full employment, saw school-leavers' aspirations as realistic, and pointed to the failings of the job placement agencies, as partly causing the phenomenon of frequent job changing.

Most of the research effort, then, after World War II focussed on the transition from school to work, with the principal objective of finding out whether the transition was smooth or beset with problems. Keil, Riddell and Green (1966), in reviewing the published work of the late 1950s and early 1960s, concluded that in general the entry into work was not traumatic, although for a minority there was a slow realisation that employment has more frustrations than

6

previously realised. It is not the purpose here to dwell too
much upon the entry to work since we are primarily concerned
with unemployment. Suffice it to say that one substantial
review bemoans the fact that a considerable amount of research
has only provided a generalised description of the
transitional years in terms of attitudes, job finding and job
changing behaviour (Clarke, 1980a). The picture is
particularly deficient in knowledge about the experience of
girls, and about the process beyond the first 18 months out of
school. A related topic was that of theories of occupational
choice, but again somewhat outside the scope of this book and
reviewed extensively elsewhere (Clarke, 1980b; West and
Newton, 1983). The key trend to note here, however, is that
it was towards the end of the 1970s that researchers began to
turn their attention to studying the effects of youth
unemployment. In one sense economic changes overtook
researchers, such that the transition from school to work was
a process occurring to an increasingly smaller proportion of
16 year old school leavers. The first few years out of school
are now characterised by a chequered pattern of experience in
youth training, in unemployment, in further education and, for
some, in employment.

On the broad front, considerable knowledge has been
acquired about psychological responses to unemployment across
different age groups (see Warr, 1984a, for a recent review).
Methodologies vary from complex longitudinal designs with
large samples to small scale case studies, but there is
convergence in demonstrating quite clearly that unemployment
causes psychological change. For the majority this is an
unpleasant deterioration in their psychological state (e.g.
Banks and Jackson, 1982; Warr and Jackson, 1985), although
for some individuals the experiences can have beneficial
effects (Fryer and Payne, 1984). Furthermore, we know
something of the differential response to unemployment as
mediated or exacerbated by such factors as sex, age, social
class, financial responsibilities, employment commitment and
social support. As to theoretical models of explanation the
literature is somewhat deficient, perhaps with the exception
of Jahoda's writings (1979, 1982), although some promising
signs are beginning to appear (Warr, 1987). Such general
achievements and strictures pertain equally to studies of
youth unemployment. However, the 16 to 19 age group are
unique because they are at a transitional stage in the life
cycle and because the youth labour market is structured quite
differently from that of the adult sector. This latter topic,
that of recent changes in the structure of the youth labour
market, is now dealt with in the following chapter.

Chapter 2

THE YOUTH LABOUR MARKET AND UNEMPLOYMENT: RECENT CHANGES

From the mid-1970s to the mid-1980s official unemployment rates in most western countries increased from around 3% to between 10% and 15%. Within each country there are wide variations around the overall rate, so that for some areas and some groups of the population 20% to 30% unemployment is not uncommon.   Teenagers, those who are older, unskilled, or previously employed in declining manufacturing industries, are particularly likely to be without jobs, as are members of ethnic minorities and disabled people.   One significant trend in recent years is the meteoric rise in unemployment amongst young people.   Between 1972 and 1977 alone unemployment among young people in Great Britain rose by 120% compared with a rise of 45% among the working population as a whole (Manpower Services Commission, 1978).

Detailed analysis of long-term trends indicates that if the unemployment rate for all males rises by one percentage point then the unemployment rate for males under 20 years old, excluding school-leavers, rises by about 1.7 percentage points (Makeham, 1980).   Changes in the unemployment rate for females under 20 are also closely related to the unemployment rate for all females; an increase of one percentage point in the former is associated with an increase of almost three percentage points in the latter. Long-term unemployment, once considered only to affect older workers, is now becoming a serious problem for young people also.   The numbers of 18-24 year olds unemployed for more than one year rose six-fold from 50,000 in 1980 to 300,000 in 1983. They now form one quarter of the long-term unemployed.

Furthermore, as part of a more general picture of disadvantage, particular groups of youth are more likely to be unemployed than others.   Most notably, the area in which a young person lives and their ethnic origin have been shown to increase the risks of unemployment (Jackson, 1985).

What was once considered to be only a temporary phenomenon now has a permanent ring to it.   One recent commentator has summed up the position:

In most countries, joblessness among the under 25s is more than twice (and in some up to 5 times) that of adults. In the seven major OECD countries, youth unemployment stood at 17% in 1983, with Italy (32%) and Britain (23%) particularly high. Ethnic minorities are also at risk. Unemployment among black 16 to 19 year olds in the U.S. has been running at more than double that for whites, as it has for adult men of West Indian (Caribbean) and Asian (Indian and Pakistani) origin in Britain.

(Thomas, 1985, p.224)

This latter author draws attention to the United States, where high youth unemployment has been a dominant issue, and where even during an era of public spending austerity youth programmes have fared better than most (Adams and Mangum, 1978; Osterman, 1981). It has been argued that the reasons for spending on youth programmes are easy to pin-point: unemployment rates for white youth were 10% at the time, and 40% for minority youth, unit costs of youth programmes were generally cheap, and helping young people was uncontroversial. Consequently, politicians were attracted to the issue and public sympathy was behind them. But despite all this there has been no clear agreement as to why youth unemployment is so high; why minority youth unemployment is even higher; what are the long-term consequences of youth unemployment; and what to do about it.

Consider for the moment how the youth labour market has changed recently. The occupational distribution of young people shows that in the early 1970s some 25% of young people entered apprenticeships and about 20% went into clerical occupations. About one-third went into jobs with little or no training. In recent years, however, traditional apprenticeships have almost disappeared and the industrial distribution of young people's jobs has been affected by a shrinkage in manufacturing and production industries, as well as by an overall reduction in the level of job opportunities. These developments have resulted in a downward shift in the career expectations and hopes of many young people.

University graduates are now competing with 18 year old school-leavers for the jobs that had come to be seen as theirs, while many 18 year olds are forced into competition with 16 year old school-leavers. One consequence of this is that many employers respond by recruiting up-market, thus eliminating the unqualified, untrained and unemployed. The employment prospects for this latter group thus become very dim indeed. It is this particular feature that resulted in Government intervention in 1978 aimed at assisting young people with reduced employment prospects.

Turning specifically to the current labour market for young people, a number of facts emerge from analysis of data

9

for 1983 and 1984. Table 2.1 gives broad estimates of the total population aged 16 and 17 in August 1983 and 1984 by what they were doing the following January. It is of interest to note the constant level of unemployment over the two years for both age groups. The main change is the fall in the 'other' category from 1984 to 1985. This category is mainly jobs outside the Youth Training Scheme and suggests that more jobs have now been brought within YTS.

Table 2.2 shows the patterns of employment of 16-17 year olds in April 1984, excluding most of those on YTS. Around three-quarters of employed males under 18 were in manual occupations, concentrated in the metal and electrical trades.

For women the position was reversed with 65% in non-manual occupations, mostly clerical and related occupations. Just under half the males under 18 and in employment were receiving formal training, but for females the proportion was below a quarter. Apprenticeship was still the dominant form of training for males (accounting for two-thirds of all in training).

Table 2.1: Education/Labour Market Status of Young People: January 1984 and January 1985, GB (thousands)

Education or Labour Market Status	Age 16[1]		Age 17[1]	
	Jan 84	Jan 85[2]	Jan 84	Jan 85[2]
Total population	895	870	915	895
Full-time education	405	395	280	285
– schools	275	270	170	170
– further education[3]	130	125	110	110
Youth Training Scheme	225	250	45[4]	40
Claimant unemployed	110	110	160	150
Other[5]	155	110	430	425

Source: Department of Employment, Department of Education and Science, MSC.

1. Ages as at 31 August of preceding year.
2. Provisional.
3. Excluding YTS.
4. Including 20,000 on the Youth Opportunities Programme.
5. Mainly those in employment outside YTS but also includes some who are seeking work but not claiming benefit, some who are neither employed nor seeking work (e.g. because of domestic responsibilities) and net errors in the other estimates.

Table 2.2: Patterns of Employment of 16-17 Year Olds, April 1984

	Males	Females
Manual occupations	76.4%	34.9%
Non-manual occupations	23.6%	65.1%
Main occupational groups (% of all occupations)	Processing, making, repairing etc. (metal and electrical) – 24% Clerical and related – 10% Selling – 9%	Clerical and related – 49% Selling – 13% Making and repairing – 10% (excl. metal and electrical)
In apprenticeship	34%	7%
In other vocational training	12%	17%
Not in training	54%	76%

Source: New Earnings Survey

Note: 'Other vocational training' is defined in the NES as including a commitment by employer and employee to a programme of training (including associated education) and work experience lasting at least 12 months.

At the macro-level of operation the two main theoretical perspectives on the youth labour market are those of human capital theory and of dual or segmented labour market theory. Human capital theory has been highly influential in terms of educational and manpower policy provision since the 1960s, and in terms of a cost-benefit exercise it has been used to estimate rates of return on investment in education and training expenditure. The theory has come in for a good deal of criticism in recent years, with its assumption about a functional relationship between education and training provision and the needs of employers for qualified manpower (Berg, 1973; Dore, 1976; Hirsch, 1983).

Dual or segmented labour market theory, in its basic form, divides jobs into primary and secondary (Gordon, 1972; Bosanquet and Doeringer, 1973). Primary jobs are characterised as needing specific qualifications and training, offering good financial rewards, high level of job satisfaction and clear prospects of a career. Jobs in the secondary labour market are basically the opposite. Little training is needed, the work is unpleasant and career prospects are non-existent. Recent analyses of the UK labour market for youth leads to the conclusion that segmented labour market theory is the most appropriate (Ashton, Maguire and Garland, 1982; Lee and Wrench, 1984). In elaborating on this basic theory a number of descriptive taxonomies have been developed to account for the mode of entry into the youth labour market. One of these describes personal histories in terms of career potential (Ashton and Field, 1976) and more recent field research has developed this into six main market segments:

    (i)   semi-skilled and unskilled manual male occupations;
    (ii) semi-skilled and unskilled manual, and lower level sales, female occupations;
   (iii) skilled male manual occupations;
   (iv) clerical female occupations;
    (v) white-collar male career occupations;
   (vi) white-collar female career occupations;

The importance of these labour market segments is in the different patterns of entry, and the way outcome is partly dependent upon competition between young people and adults (Ashton and Maguire, 1986). In a later publication the same authors emphasise the role of area differences in the pattern of entry to the youth labour market, and the exclusion from large parts of the labour market of 18 year olds who have not obtained a formal training (Ashton and Maguire, 1986).

Related to the work of Ashton and colleagues is that of Lee and Wrench (1984), who suggest four types of bridge from school into the contemporary labour market. These are termed

the super-privileged route, the extra-privileged route, the
privileged route and the under-privileged route. The four
categories appear to represent a continuum of occupational
status and earning potential. The super-privileged route
offers either higher education or professional training on the
job, whilst the other three types involved direct entry from
school into the labour market. The extra-privileged route
offers extended vocational training leading to credentials and
a skilled occupation. The privileged route still offers some
vocational training but less than the previous route. It does
offer, however, a good prospect of regular employment in, for
example, low grade white collar work and in retailing. As the
name suggests, the under-privileged route promises bleaker
prospects, typically involving periods of unemployment, short-
term and part-time work. It is characterised by uncertainty,
insecurity and disadvantage in the labour market. The route
in its early phase would also offer participation in youth
training schemes.
    The descriptive taxonomies here outlined have common
characteristics to some extent, but in general their value
lies in the extension of dual labour market theory to a multi-
level system.
    It seems likely that early labour market careers of 16
year old school leavers are now grouped into four main types:
(i) the increasingly rare cases of a smooth transition from
education into employment, (ii) those who progress from
education via vocational training schemes into primary sector
jobs, (iii) those who move through special measures and
unemployment into secondary sector jobs, and (iv) those who
descend quite rapidly into long term unemployment. It is this
latter group, and to a lesser extent the third group, who are
the major concern in this book.
    In the United Kingdom, as in other European countries,
the rising youth unemployment rates led to the introduction of
special measures aimed at alleviating the effects of
unemployment. In 1977 there was a combination of rather small
scale measures directed at the problem of youth unemployment.
These included short training courses, Job Creation Schemes,
the Work Experience Programme and Community Industry. They
were largely designed to offset the reductions in craft
apprenticeships and technicians' traineeships caused by the
recession.
    Then in 1978 there was the publication of the Holland
Report (Manpower Services Commission, 1978). This was the
result of an MSC working party set up to study the feasibility
of a training and work experience programme for 16-18 year
olds. Their proposals aimed to bring the somewhat disjointed
existing provisions together within a co-ordinated programme.
The new programme was known as the Youth Opportunities
Programme (YOP), and was aimed mainly at the unqualified and
least able, hoping to give them a foot-hold onto the

13

employment ladder. In addition to providing training and work experience, YOP also aimed to improve motivation, attitudes and social skills. It is also significant that YOP was a provision for unemployed young people, with no real integration with normal employment.

The overall impact of YOP on the youth labour market between 1978 and 1982 can be summed up under four headings:

(i) First, the effect on the level of youth employment was modest, since more jobs may have been lost through substitution than were gained as a result of YOP places. Furthermore the labour market collapsed substantially in 1979, not helping the objectives of YOP.

(ii) Second, YOP reduced the level of registered youth unemployment, by withdrawing young people from the official figures. This achievement is not to be scorned; most young people much preferred YOP to unemployment.

(iii) Third, YOP had some marginal effect in redistributing youth unemployment, away from the more disadvantaged.

(iv) And fourth, where YOP did help young people find employment it usually did so through its effect on employers' recruitment practices (Raffe, 1984).

By 1981 criticism of YOP was becoming increasingly widespread and based upon the poor employment prospects of ex-trainees, the low level of allowance, accusations of exploitation of young people as cheap labour, and, most important, the lack of quality of training. As part of a wider consultative exercise under the title A New Training Initiative, vocational preparation for young people was once again seriously re-examined (Manpower Services Commission, 1981a). The eventual result of this consultation was the Youth Training Scheme (YTS). This was a higher quality scheme, lasting up to one year, offering work experience, a minimum of three months off-the-job training and providing for induction, assessment, guidance and counselling. It is essentially a training scheme, encompassing both employed and unemployed young people. It is drawing in substantial numbers of 16 year old school leavers and from 1985-6 YTS has been extended to a two year scheme. It will cater for about 360,000 entrants in 1986/87, constituted roughly as follows:

85% of unemployed 16 year olds
50% of employed 16 year olds
60-65% of unemployed 17 year old school leavers
40% of employed 17 year old school leavers

In late 1982 the Community Programme was introduced to increase the job creation scope for the long-term unemployed, who are out of the range of YTS (i.e. 18 and over).   It provides 130,000 places (1 in 10 of the target population) and it is planned to extend this by a further 100,000.   Much of the employment is intended to be part-time, and hourly wages are supposed to comply with rate for the job.   Overall, it is designed to make participants better off than if they were on the dole.   The majority of participants are 18-25 year olds and unmarried.

One of the best guides to the current overall picture for post-16 destinations comes from the national Youth Cohort Study, which is a representative sample of 16-19 year olds in England and Wales (Jones, Gray and Clough, 1987; Clough, Gray and Jones, 1987).   Immediately after the fifth form, in 1984, 10% were unemployed.   Over the following year about half of these remained unemployed, a quarter transferred to YTS and 17% found a job.   There was, however, a corresponding inflow to the unemployed group during this period, so that the percentage unemployed in 1985 was also around 10%.   And one year after reaching the minimum school leaving age 27% were still at school or in sixth form colleges, 24% were in a full-time job and 23% were on YTS.   The overall impression of this year was one of stability, with 4 in 5 remaining in the same status (Jones, Gray and Clough, 1987).

Chapter 3

YOUTH UNEMPLOYMENT: A BRIEF OVERVIEW OF RECENT RESEARCH

Recent research on the topic of youth unemployment and the youth labour market can be divided into four themes.   These are:

1.   The extent to which socio-demographic characteristics of youth and of their backgrounds shape aspirations, expectations and plans concerning education and employment.   Within this theme typically are to be found studies of the role of educational attainment, social class background, gender and ethnicity in influencing success in the labour market.

2.   Analysis of the structure of and processes operating in the youth labour market.   Included here are analyses of young people's knowledge about and perceptions of the labour market, the role of education and careers counselling in preparing young people for employment, job search behaviour and the impact of state intervention.   Also included are studies of the demand side, i.e. employer recruitment strategies.

3.   A third identifiable theme concerns the social-psychological consequences of unemployment and early career.   There is now a considerable literature on issues such as the impact of unemployment on psychological distress, self-esteem and the work ethic.   Research has also been concerned to identify factors that moderate the impact, such as social support systems and attributions for the cause of unemployment.

4.   Fourth, there are studies of the behavioural consequences of different labour market experiences. Of interest here are analyses of the connections between high youth unemployment levels and increased crime, delinquency, extremist politics, substance abuse and other forms of anti-social behaviour.

16

Youth Unemployment: A Brief Overview of Recent Research

This chapter seeks to provide a brief overview of research on these four themes and in subsequent chapters the literature, particularly on well-being and on attachment to the labour market, is examined in much greater detail as appropriate to interpretation of results from the present study.

1. SOCIO-DEMOGRAPHIC CHARACTERISTICS AND THE LABOUR MARKET

Arguably the research to have had most impact within this theme is that based on cultural reproduction theory (Willis, 1977; Jenkins, 1983). The key issue here has been to explain the dynamics of how children from working class backgrounds remain in that position after leaving school. The method of explanation relies heavily on establishing links between the culture of the school and the culture of the shop-floor, through the ideologies of masculinity, anti-authoritarianism and the celebration of manual labour.

Cultural reproduction theory, with its often dense exposition and cursory empirical support, has little to say about middle-class youth or indeed about what happens after entering the labour market. One attempt to describe the stratification of educational and employment opportunities has been through the status attainment model (e.g. Breen, 1984). This approach demonstrated the importance of sex and class background in determining school leaving, which in turn determines the segment of the labour market entered.

Although historically there has been a tendency in the literature to focus almost exclusively on male unemployment, thus tacitly implying that women are only supplementary wage earners (Liem and Rayman, 1984), there are compelling recent data documenting the growth in female participation in the labour force (e.g. Martin and Roberts, 1984), and identifying the consequences of unemployment for young women (e.g. Stafford, Jackson and Banks, 1980; Banks and Jackson, 1982; Warr, Banks and Ullah, 1985). The majority of girls leaving school now can expect to be employed outside the home for a good part of their future, and their income will be a major factor, if not the sole factor, in influencing their family's economic well-being. As a consequence the role of women's early experiences of unemployment and the labour market in shaping their lives and personalities is a crucially important research question.

Another major socio-demographic category influencing youth's entry into the labour market is ethnicity. Discrimination combined with the concentration of ethnic minorities in economically run-down areas means that coloured youth enter inferior quality jobs and experience more unemployment than their white counterparts. Considerable evidence exists on this topic which, together with the

17

literature on sex differences, is covered more fully in Chapter 5. Although not directly relevant to this present study it is nonetheless important to acknowledge here the impact also of family background and school environment factors in influencing point of entry to the labour market (e.g. Rosier, 1978).

2. THE STRUCTURE OF THE YOUTH LABOUR MARKET

To study the way in which youth first confront the labour market, then to be subsequently sorted into a range of early careers, is not easy. Yet an understanding of the structure and dynamics of the youth labour market is one of the basics to furthering our knowledge of socialisation during late adolescence and early adulthood.

Economists have tended to contribute to our comprehension of the youth labour market at the macro-level, by engaging in the debate about dual (Doeringer and Piore, 1971) and segmented (Lee and Wrench, 1984) labour markets. Put quite simply, early school leavers, along with some other identifiable groups such as blacks and women returning to work, can only expect to find jobs in the secondary sector. This is characterised by lower wages, job insecurity, little training and poor working conditions. The need to refine the youth labour market into differentiated sectors has been further underlined by Ashton, Maguire and Garland (1982), who examined the recruitment policies of representative samples of employers in different labour markets. Whilst these approaches have helped to clarify how the market operates in general terms, they are of limited value to psychologists seeking to understand individual careers and motivations, particularly as they vary within broad socio-demographic groups.

Questions posed by psychologists in this area tend to focus on job search behaviour and attitudes to employment. Concern has been expressed about the level of job-seeking behaviour and the intention to work of young people, and in particular how prolonged spells of unemployment may create reduced levels of both. The problem is seen as being more acute among young unemployed blacks of Afro-Caribbean descent, where the hypothesised causal influence of unemployment on alienation has achieved the status of conventional wisdom (Gaskell and Smith, 1981). In fact, the evidence is rather thin. A few studies have concentrated on the factors associated with job separation (e.g. Baxter, 1975; Cherry, 1976; Raffe, 1983), while others have looked more specifically at the differences in job-seeking behaviour between blacks and whites (e.g. Commission for Racial Equality, 1978; Dex, 1979). Roberts, Noble and Duggan (1982b), addressing the issue of labour market withdrawal, suggest there is a voluntary component to youth unemployment, such that jobs are not sought particularly strenuously during longer periods of unemployment, as a means of avoiding rejections and thereby protecting self-esteem. Furthermore, the psychological mechanism by which this adjustment occurs is likely to involve a number of mediating variables, such as expectations (Feather, 1982; Feather and Davenport, 1981) and attitudes to looking for work (Ullah and Banks, 1985). This question of labour market attachment forms a significant part of the research project reported in this book, and the literature is dealt with more fully in Chapter 7.

3.   THE SOCIAL AND PSYCHOLOGICAL CONSEQUENCES OF UNEMPLOYMENT

Considerable research effort has gone into exploring the relationships between unemployment and health, which has been concisely reviewed by Warr (1984;   1985). His conclusions can be summarised quite briefly. Individual level studies (such as Kasl, Gore and Cobb, 1975; Kasl and Cobb, 1980; Wilder, 1980; Cook, Cummins, Bartley and Shaper, 1982; Verbrugge, 1983) produce conflicting evidence, such that it is not possible to say whether or not unemployment directly causes impaired physical health. Aggregate level studies of economic change and mortality (such as Brenner, 1971, 1973, 1979, 1980 a and b; Brenner and Mooney, 1982) are intriguing and suggestive, not least because they use time-series data, but taken on their own they do not permit conclusions on the causal impact of recession on mortality. Ambivalent findings are also produced from research on economic change and health services utilisation (such as Brenner, 1973; Catalano, Dooley and Jackson, 1981; Stokes and Cochrane, 1984). Research on economic conditions and suicide has a long history, but even so authors are agreed that there is no clear evidence of a causal link (Warr, 1984b; Platt, 1984). Individual level cross-sectional studies indicate that suicides occur more among the unemployed than the employed (Platt, 1984), but over time the same personal and environmental factors may have operated to produce both the unemployment and the suicide (Shepherd and Barraclough, 1980). Studies of para-suicide again reveal high rates among the unemployed, but interviews with survivors rarely point to unemployment as the major precipitating factor (Platt and Kreitman, 1985).

In turning to research on unemployment and psychological well-being, however, conclusions appear to be much clearer, based on extensive individual level studies, both cross-sectional and longitudinal. Cross-sectional comparisons of groups of employed and unemployed have typically shown increased psychological distress, depression and anxiety, less happiness, lowered self-esteem and a greater experience of strain amongst the unemployed (a thorough review of this

19

literature is to be found in Warr, 1985). More important, recent longitudinal research has identified greater impairment as a result of unemployment, and also significant improvements after re-employment (e.g. Banks and Jackson, 1982; Jackson, Stafford, Banks and Warr, 1983; Warr and Jackson, 1985). A number of processes have been incorporated in a model accounting for responses to unemployment. These include reduced income, restriction of behaviour and environment, goal structure, reduced scope for decision-making and skill-utilisation, increase in threatening activities (such as job search leading to rejection), reduced interpersonal contact and changed social position (Warr, 1987). Furthermore, empirical research has found a number of factors (such as employment commitment, social support, age, local unemployment rate) that mediate the impact of unemployment. In comprehending reactions to unemployment both these sets of factors, that is processes and mediators, need to be considered.

Looking specifically at youth unemployment, the literature provides us with a varied and somewhat incomplete picture of what happens to 16 to 19 year olds who find themselves unemployed. In Chapter 6 research on unemployment and adolescent well-being is reviewed fully, including the dimensions of general distress, depression, anxiety, self-esteem, stigma and mood states. At the same time attention has also focussed on the work ethic and on attributional styles (Feather, 1982; Furnham, 1984), in themselves or as moderators of well-being outcomes. The role of social supports in buffering the impact of unemployment has also received attention (Ullah, Banks and Warr, 1985). Despite some contributions (e.g. Roberts, Noble and Duggan, 1984) on the whole sociologists have not been too forthcoming with empirical material on the consequences of youth unemployment.

4. BEHAVIOURAL CONSEQUENCES OF UNEMPLOYMENT

If the concepts referred to in section 3 above can be inferred from interview and questionnaire responses, then a final set of research questions can be described as concerning directly observable behaviours. Crime and delinquency are among the most frequently discussed outcomes of unemployment, although Grainger (1980) concluded that there is no simple or direct relationship. One major American longitudinal study found unemployed youth to report twice as much use of illicit drugs and aggressive acts as did the employed (Bachman, O'Malley and Johnston, 1978). However, although widely cited, this later study suffers from only including men and from infrequent data collection points, so that causal inference is made difficult. More broadly, there is a consensus in the literature, as identified by Freeman and Medoff (1982), that crime may be an alternative for youth who cannot find paid employment.

Generally speaking, little is known about how social activities change over time and are affected by continuing unemployment.   One study (Turtle and Ridley, 1984) found that the longer term unemployed spent more time drinking alone, less time playing sports, slept more during the day and lost contact with friends. But times have changed, and many youths recognise the inevitability of early unemployment or at least intermittent employment.   The question of the social-behavioural outcomes of unemployment is therefore an important one.   In particular, gender differences are worthy of study not least because sex-role socialisation is both likely to be create different responses to unemployment and in turn to affected by unemployment. Whilst some young women may strive even harder for success in the labour market to escape the traditional domestic role as a fall-back, the pressures for some may be too strong to resist.   Female experiences have received some attention (e.g. Stafford, Jackson and Banks, 1980; Griffin, 1985a and b; Coffield, Borrill and Marshall, 1986) but the picture is woefully inadequate.   Similarly, the relationship between youth and their families, with all but a few exceptions (e.g. Coffield et al., 1983), has received scant attention, despite its importance as a source of job vacancy information and as a means of social support (Ullah, Banks and Warr, 1985).   Of crucial importance in this respect is the role played by money, or more accurately, the lack of it, in establishing independence or in maintaining dependence on parents.   It appears from the literature that, although more free time is available, young unemployed people become more socially isolated, with a home-centred, privatised kind of leisure pattern (O'Brien and Kabanoff, 1979; Coffield et al., 1983).

A further behavioural outcome to have attracted attention is that of political radicalism, although not as much atten-tion as one might expect from the potentially explosive nature of the topic.   Since unemployment can be considered as a political issue, collective responses might be considered to include political involvement.   Yet the literature suggests that the unemployed are not mobilised as a political force because they are offered no ideologies linking their personal predicament to political action (Schlozman and Verba, 1979).   Studies specifically of young people indicate that there is considerable disenchantment with the mainstream political system (Breakwell, 1986; Banks and Ullah, 1987), and that the young unemployed express verbal attitudes in favour of direct political action, lawbreaking and violent change (Clark, 1985; Gaskell and Smith, 1985; Breakwell, 1986).   To what extent such attitudes are translated into action is less clear (Jackson, 1985).

Chapter 4

THE PRESENT RESEARCH

1. RECENT BACKGROUND AND OBJECTIVES

As described in Chapter 2 recent rapid increases in
unemployment have fallen disproportionately upon certain
groups in society; young people are one such group, the more
so if they are poorly qualified and from ethnic minorities.
Alongside rising unemployment, recent years have seen a
considerable growth in youth training (under the Manpower
Services Commission) and a drying up of youth jobs and
apprenticeships, such that we are now witnessing widespread
dislocation in the traditional labour market structures for
young people leaving school.

The fact that unemployment has a negative impact on young
people has been established in a number of studies, although
the evidence needs to be qualified with statements about
sampling biases, the year of investigation, adequacy of
measures and broader theoretical issues. Although the general
finding of a deleterious impact of unemployment has been
corroborated in a number of studies, there is a clear need to
investigate differential responses, specifying the factors and
processes that mediate unemployment effects and the
circumstances under which effects may or may not be observed.

In this context and in the wake of the deepening
recession of the late 1970s, this present longitudinal study
of the social and psychological effects of youth unemployment
was commissioned by the Department of Employment in 1981, and
fieldwork began in 1982.

Since no study can adequately answer all the important
questions about responses to youth unemployment, choices were
made among the priorities in order to avoid an over-general
project. Thus this study concentrated on poorly qualified 16
year old school leavers, largely inner city urban dwellers,
and compared blacks (of Afro-Caribbean descent) with whites.
Other conditions defining the sample are explained in greater
detail later, but the major objectives of studying this target
group are now set out:

22

(i)   Particular attention was paid to identifying and measuring the so-called 'discouraged worker effect'. For example, do young people who spend long periods out of work early in their post-school life show reduced levels of employment commitment, and do they withdraw from the labour market? What is the association between duration of unemployment and labour market attitudes? Is such an effect (if there is one) reversible, once young people subsequently become employed?

(ii)   A second major objective was to see whether long spells of unemployment (up to two and a half years) were related to lower psychological well-being. Rather surprisingly, previous studies, though of less adequate samples, have found this not to be the case; neither has there been found to be a correlation between well-being and proportion of time spent unemployed. It may be that young people adapt to a state of unemployment, so that it gradually comes to lose its deleterious impact; or the association may have been masked by other factors in earlier studies. In either case the issue is of substantial importance and by taking detailed career histories since leaving school it was explored in full. Alongside measures of psychological well-being this study also included measures of general health, of health service utilisation and of personality.

(iii)   Associated with the preceding two issues this study also explored the importance of social networks, supports and pressures in determining the form of psychological response to unemployment. For example, what types of social support developed to sustain morale and mental health in the absence of work? Did norms within social networks contribute or not to a reduction in employment commitment? Which categories of young people were likely to be members of particular social networks?

(iv)   Throughout the study especial attention is paid to differences between males and females, and between blacks and whites. The importance of these differences is reflected in the sampling strategy, which was chosen specifically to ensure adequate members in each of these categories.

(v)   The final objective incorporated a number of themes of importance in understanding young people's response to unemployment. These included the nature of employment and training being sought, the methods of job search, perceptions of

> discrimination, experience of special measures, activities whilst unemployed, political attitudes and voting, and financial deprivation.

2. DESIGN OF THE STUDY

It is frequently the case in quasi-experimental designs (such as are described in Cook and Campbell, 1976) that researchers have to consider carefully the advantages and disadvantages of different sampling strategies. This requirement of course applies to all research relying on a form of sampling, but in our case the issue mainly centres around the trade-off between internal validity and external validity (Kasl, 1982). Good internal validity is to be found in highly targeted sampling where strong causal inference can be made, whereas good external validity is associated with findings that can be generalised to larger populations. Some studies, with resources sufficient to allow the selection of very large samples, can successfully result in high validity on both counts, but most field projects end up with some kind of compromise. In the case of sampling young people four principal strategies are available. These are:

- surveys of households
- school leaver records
- registers of the unemployed
- targeted samples with defined characteristics

Household surveys, whilst in theory having the advantage of enabling a fully representative sample to be achieved, are very costly to mount. In particular, when searching for sub-groups of households with well defined characteristics such as unemployed youth, the necessary over-sampling is costly indeed. More generally, household surveys often ignore non-urban areas and also have problems in defining exactly what constitutes a household. How, for example, does one deal with residential hostels for young people?

Samples based on school leaver or fifth form lists provide the best opportunity for representative sampling, but also suffer some disadvantages of household surveys. For example, they are also costly if one is interested only in a sub-population, and if a national sample is contemplated, to obtain local authority permissions is a time consuming business. Lists can also be inaccurate, out of date and deficient in respect of movers in and out of the area, especially if contact is initiated post-16.

Sampling from the unemployment register clearly misses those non-registered young people, but in addition creates the practical problem of obtaining permissions from the Department of Employment and the Department of Health and Social

24

Security. Such permission to release names and addresses is not easy to obtain, even if the project is funded from central government.

The fourth sampling strategy is to deliberately target a sample with certain individual and group characteristics. In the present field study it was not the purpose to produce aggregate estimates of, for example, unemployment durations. This is likely to vary from year to year, from place to place, according to labour demand, provision of special youth programmes and so on. To study such phenomena requires systematic representative sampling. Rather, the main purpose of the study, in strategic terms, was analytic and explanatory (i.e. searching for causal relationships) with the inclusion of some purely descriptive information. Key target groups were Afro-Caribbeans and whites, males and females, urban dwellers and those with few educational qualifications. The ethnic group and educational qualifications factor were also related to the requirement that we study those more at risk for longer-term unemployment. Hence, the sampling strategy was one that is high on internal validity and less high on external validity. Even so, the sample is representative of unemployed urban youth, of black and white ethnic groups, and with few educational qualifications. Consequently, the analytic conclusions will apply to a population defined by those characteristics, or to sub-groups therein.

The study was designed as a two stage longitudinal survey. The first round of interviews took place in 1982, approximately a year after the sample left school (referred to as time one or t1), and the second stage (referred to as time two or t2) occurred one year later. The second stage was designed to follow up all the young people interviewed at time one, whether they were currently unemployed or employed at time two. In addition, it was decided to undertake first-time interviews at time two with a boost sample of unemployed people. This procedure was adopted in order to compensate for the inevitable non-response at follow-up, therefore providing a sufficiently large base for analysis within each segment of the time two sample, particularly those experiencing extensive periods of unemployment.

Throughout the study fieldwork and initial coding was carried out by MAS Survey Research Ltd., on behalf of the Social and Applied Psychology Unit. Full technical reports on both stages have been produced by MAS[1].

3. THE SAMPLES

The sample was defined as young men and women who left school during 1982 at the minimum school leaving age of 16, with a maximum of two CSE Grade 1 or 'O' level passes, who had been

25

currently registered as unemployed for at least four weeks prior to interview and who were not registered as disabled.

3.1 Time One Sample

At the commencement of fieldwork the plan was to obtain 400 each of white females, white males, black females and black males, the blacks being of Afro-Caribbean descent whatever their place of birth. This total sample of 1600 was to be drawn from 10 urban areas, with the same proportion in each area of males and females, whites and blacks.

However, despite the strenuous efforts of MAS Survey Research Limited, difficulty was experienced in recruiting the planned sample of young blacks. The final sample of black respondents was achieved by relaxing some of the contacting restrictions, enlarging the geographical areas of contact and introducing an eleventh area.

The number of completed interviews by area, sex and group is shown in Table 4.1. It can be seen that the total achieved sample was 1150, consisting of 388 white males, 388 white females, 245 black males and 129 black females. Fifty five per cent had no educational qualifications, 34% had CSEs and 10% had 'O' levels. There were no sex or ethnic group differences in educational qualifications.

The strict conditions of admission to the sample meant that only 10% of those approached by interviewers were in fact eligible. Of those contacted and eligible, agreement and completed interviews were obtained from 70%. The main reasons for refusing to be interviewed were: not enough time, too busy, and not interested. In addition a number of appointments were not kept. Information about non-responding is provided in Table 4.3.

3.2 Time Two Follow-up Sample

In respect of the follow-up of time one interviewees, the total number of addresses available was 1140 (the shortfall resulted from ten 1982 Check Letters being returned as 'not known'), from which 73% completed interviews were achieved. This is a response rate of 64% on addresses available.

The fieldwork was divided into two periods, since follow-up interviews were designed to be undertaken as near as possible to one year after the time one interview. The first set of follow-up interviews was carried out between June 10th and July 2nd 1983, whilst the second group was carried out between August 30th and September 17th 1983. The number of follow-up interviews achieved in each area is shown in the left-hand section of Table 4.2.

Of those 732 people re-interviewed at time two, three in ten were found to be in employment. Although there was an ethnic difference in employment rates (26.3% among blacks,

Table 4.1: Completed Interviews at Time One by Area, Sex and Ethnic Group

Area Number	Name	White Males	White Females	Black Males	Black Females	Totals
01	Greater Manchester	46	43	47	23	159
02	Merseyside	42	40	18	13	113
03	West Yorkshire	40	40	51	31	162
04	South Yorkshire	40	42	13	11	106
05	Nottingham/Leicester	43	40	18	10	111
06	West Midlands	41	40	61	19	161
07	Bristol	41	41	1	1	84
08	Slough/Luton/Reading/Bedford	43	40	18	5	106
09	Lewisham/North Kent	18	36	7	8	69
10a	Willesden	13	12	11	7	43
11	South Essex	21	14	—	1	36
	Totals	388	388	245	129	1150

Table 4.2: Completed Interviews at Stage Two of the Study, Summarized by Area

| | Follow-up Interviews | | | | Boost Interviews | | | | Full Sample | | | |
| | Black | | White | | Black | | White | | Black | | White | |
	Male	Female	Male	Female	Male	Female	Male	Female	Male	Female	Male	Female
01 Manchester	27	12	35	24	19	20	11	17	46	32	46	41
02 Liverpool	8	5	29	28	4	7	14	16	12	12	43	44
03 Leeds	38	22	30	28	14	10	13	11	52	32	43	39
04 Sheffield	7	7	29	32	33	28	20	13	40	35	49	45
05 Nottingham	14	8	25	28	24	18	15	12	38	26	40	40
06 Birmingham	41	14	30	26	10	28	17	20	51	42	47	46
07 Bristol	1	1	27	22	0	0	22	18	1	1	49	40
08 Slough/Luton	11	1	29	23	7	2	20	20	18	3	49	43
09 London A	4	5	13	24	27	6	27	14	31	11	40	38
10 London B	1	0	2	3	0	0	0	0	1	0	2	3
11 S.E. Essex	0	1	13	9	0	0	0	0	0	1	13	9
Totals	152	76	262	247	138	119	159	141	290	195	421	388

31.7% among whites), this was almost entirely due to the low rate among black males (23.8%). The proportions employed amongst the other three groups were very similar: 30.1% for black females, 31.3% for white males, and 32.1% for white females.

Table 4.3: Reasons for Non-response at Time Two Interviews in the Follow-up Sample

	N	%
Not known at address/no such address	69	6
Moved house	142	12
Unable to contact for other reasons	159	14
Refused to be interviewed	38	3
Re-interviewed	732	64
Addresses issued	1140	100

The structure of the initial sample in terms of sex and ethnic group at time one is shown in Table 4.4 together with details of the time two re-interview sample (i.e. excluding the boost respondents). It can be seen that there was very little difference in sample composition at time one and at re-interview.

Table 4.4: Composition of the Sample at Time One and the Follow-up Sample at Time Two

	Black		White		Total	
	T1	T2	T1	T2	T1	T2
Male	245	151	388	259	633	410
	(21%)	(21%)	(34%)	(35%)	(55%)	(56%)
Female	129	73	388	249	517	322
	(11%)	(10%)	(34%)	(34%)	(45%)	(44%)
Total	374	224	776	508	1150	732

29

3.3   Time Two Boost Sample

The criteria for entry to the boost sample were drawn up so as to make the follow-up and the boost samples as equivalent as possible. Thus the boost sample comprised unemployed young men and women who had left school during 1981 at the minimum school leaving age of 16, with a maximum of two CSE Grade 1 or 'O' level passes, who were not registered disabled, and who had been, at the time of contact, unemployed for at least four weeks. The requirement to be registered as unemployed was dropped, since it was expected that not all of the follow-up sample would be registered at the time of their re-interview. The total number of achieved interviews was 550. Approximate details by area and sub-group are given in the middle columns of Table 4.2.

4.   FIELDWORK PROCEDURE

A pilot study of 15 interviews was carried out in May 1982 in West Yorkshire using four interviewers. As a result several amendments to the questionnaire were made, resulting in a shorter version. In view of the contacting problems which had emerged, a less restrictive procedure was recommended for the main survey.

In the main time one survey, carried out between June and October 1982, it was required that at least half the respondents should be contacted outside Unemployment Benefit Offices, and up to one quarter at Careers Offices; the remainder could be contacted in other locations. Interviews were carried out as soon as possible after contact was made. Thirty-four percent of interviews were conducted in interviewers' cars, 16% in respondents' homes, and the remaining half in a variety of locations (e.g. cafes, careers offices, parks).

The same sampling points were used for the boost as were used in the 1982 survey, except that London B and S.E. Essex were excluded. In addition no interviews with blacks were attempted in Bristol, as there was still considerable unrest in certain areas of the city.

The basic procedure used at time one was again used, in that contacting was concentrated at Unemployment Benefit Offices and Careers Offices; interviewers carried letters of authority, as before, for managers of Unemployment Benefit Offices and Careers Offices, and for respondents. However, because of the difficulty in recruitment in 1982, some contacting also took place in youth clubs, hostels for the young, unemployed centres, and shopping centres. In addition, potential contacts for the boost sample were identified from information supplied by members of the follow-up sample.

As with the follow-up, the boost interviewing was carried out in two phases: between July 9th and 23rd, and between

September 24th and 30th 1983. This enabled the drop-out from each phase of the follow-up interviews to be replaced at the correct time. After the second set of boost interviews a special effort was made to obtain further interviews with black respondents in areas where fruitful contacting places had been identified. This additonal boost fieldwork took place from October 31st to November 5th 1983.

The total sample size achieved at time two, follow-up and boost together, was 1282. It can be seen from the right-hand column of Table 4.2 that the final shortfall was primarily of black females. However, on an area basis, there were relatively low numbers of black interviewees of both sexes in Liverpool, Bristol, Slough/Luton, London and S.E. Essex.

In addition to these sampling differences, the time two fieldwork was more complex than at time one because three questionnaires had to be used. Within the follow-up sample, separate questionnaires were needed for respondents who were employed and unemployed. The third questionnaire was for the boost interviews.

NOTES

1   MAS Survey Research Ltd. (1982) Youth Unemployment Survey Technical Report: JN 3584.

MAS Survey Research Ltd. (1984) 1983 Youth Unemployment Surveys, Technical Report and Documentation: JN 3983/4/5/6.

The achieved sample of white respondents was very close to the target.

Chapter 5

DISADVANTAGED YOUTH AND EARLY CAREERS

It is widely accepted that young people's experience of
unemployment and the labour market is markedly different from
that of adults (for example, Makeham, 1980; Ashton, Maguire
and Garland, 1982).   The youth labour market differs from the
adult labour market in terms of job types, entry patterns and
selection criteria, whilst the experience of unemployment for
those who have never or only fleetingly held a job is to be
expected to be different from that of, say, middle aged
redundant workers.   Furthermore, young people change jobs
more frequently and are at greater risk of being unemployed
(Daniel, 1974; Daniel and Stilgoe, 1977).

> The one factor that did emerge as of overwhelming
> importance with regard to the experiences, behaviour and
> attitudes of the unemployment was age.
>
> (Daniel and Stilgoe, 1977, p.156)

From national data collected in 1973 Daniel and Stilgoe (1977)
showed that the picture of the young unemployed was that of a
group who held jobs for short periods of time, gave them up
because they did not like them, were relatively quickly able
to find new ones, and consequently suffered only relatively
short periods of unemployment.   Furthermore, the same authors
found that older workers, regardless of their level of skill,
training, qualifications, or sex, had more difficulty in
finding jobs, took longer to find them, when they were
successful the jobs were not as good as their previous ones,
and they were more likely to drop out of the labour market.
Since the early 1970s, however, job vacancies have dried
up and job-changing as a normal response to combat boredom in
low-level jobs now results in more frequent and prolonged
periods of unemployment.   For a sizeable number the shrinkage
in vacancies also means that they will not enter a first job
at all during the years immediately after school leaving.
The research literature on labour market experiences of
young people has tended to concentrate on those who change

jobs frequently (for example, Phillips, 1973; Baxter, 1975; Cherry, 1976), or on unemployment (for example, Donovan and Oddy, 1982; Stafford, Jackson and Banks, 1980). Even in longitudinal designs the tendency is to use change in employment status from one time to another as an indicator of labour market activity (Banks and Jackson, 1982; Tiggemann and Winefield, 1984). This approach is necessary for some purposes and has contributed to our understanding of unemployment effects, but it could potentially be improved by considering labour market experience as a dynamic concept. Cross-sectional accounts represent snapshots of what is, in truth, a constantly changing pattern. Such indices fail to portray the flow into and out of the pool of unemployed. In contrast, personal histories taken at successive points in time provide a means of representing change. Some empirical studies have achieved this (Dex, 1983), whilst there are cogent theoretical arguments supporting the use of personal histories in both the youth labour market (Ashton and Field, 1976) and in the adult labour market (Nicholson, 1984).

It is an important point to emphasize that the employed and the unemployed are in many cases the same people at different points in time. Both Townsend (1979) and Roberts, Duggan and Noble (1981) point out, in different ways, that early careers are unsatisfactorily captured as employed or unemployed. Rather, there is a spectrum of experience ranging from permanent secure employment to continuous unemployment. And very often the typical youngster at the centre of our study has a career falling somewhere in between these two extremes.

Even under current economic conditions there is still considerable movement of individuals between special government training schemes and unemployment, as well as a moderate degree of mobility in and out of jobs. The analysis of such changes is of interest per se, and also as a major independent variable in assessing the social and psychological effects of unemployment.

1. JOB-CHANGING AND LABOUR MARKET EXPERIENCE

Many early studies pointed to a normative pattern of job-changing amongst school leavers - it was common, voluntary, and generally not damaging to the individual (Maizels, 1970; Carter, 1969; Baxter, 1975; Cherry, 1976). This pattern is typical of the secondary labour market. Maizels (1970) cites 50% of boys and 60% of girls having left their first jobs after two years in the labour market. Carter (1969) reported that one third of his sample had changed jobs before the end of the first year. And Cherry (1976) reported that 56% of boys and 66% of girls changed jobs in the first three years out of school.

One important question concerns the meaning of job-changing. Such evidence as is available suggests that although extreme job-changing may be associated with personal problems there was no evidence of it leading to occupational problems. So it can be seen as both symptomatic of the secondary labour market and as a developmental process of testing out, floundering or crystallisation as predicted by theories of vocational choice (eg. Ginzberg, Ginsberg, Axelrad and Herma, 1951; Super, 1957). The concepts in vocational choice theory have attracted criticism from those who fail to detect deliberate choice in the behaviour of most 16 year old leavers, instead preferring to see the process of entry and change as one of occupational allocation (Roberts, 1971). In reality neither position is likely to be completely accurate, and any theory applicable to this age group and sector of the labour market has to come to terms with two more or less established facts. One is the relative frequency, as described above, of job changing. The second is the fact that most such jobs in the secondary labour market are boring and bereft of satisfaction. They are careerless and the young person then changes jobs to add variety to their life or to maximize the instrumental rewards (e.g. Ashton and Field, 1976). Analysis of the United States labour market suggests that subsequently young people move from the secondary to the primary labour market in the search for job security and opportunities for advancement (Osterman, 1981). However, this movement appears to have little credence in the United Kingdom, and instead the segmentation determined by educational qualifications appears to largely influence the long term trajectory of people's careers. Transfer from the secondary to the primary labour market rarely occurs.

2. UNEMPLOYMENT AND SEX DIFFERENCES

Up until recently the research literature on unemployment had concentrated mainly on the experience of men, largely because female unemployment was considered less important, in both the quantitative and the qualitative sense. Women have been socialized to carry out unpaid domestic labour, whilst at the same time forming a reserve army of labour from which employers could draw at times of high demand (McIntosh, 1979), and many women without a job do not register as unemployed, even though they may be looking for employment. One outstanding exception to this trend is the recent large survey of over 5000 women of working age (Martin and Roberts, 1984), in which it was demonstrated that non-working women can be located on a continuum from unemployment to permanent economic activity, their exact position changing as their marital and child-bearing/rearing circumstances change. Turning to young women in particular we find that the little evidence that is available suggests that they have a greater risk of unemployment than young males (Manpower Services Commission, 1978; Stafford, Jackson and Banks, 1980). The issue of female youth unemployment therefore is equally deserving of study.

3. UNEMPLOYMENT AND ETHNICITY

There is consistently strong evidence to suggest that the probability of experiencing unemployment is much greater for blacks than for whites (Smith, 1976, 1981; Stafford, Jackson and Banks, 1980; Becker and Hills, 1981; Marks, 1981; Dex, 1982, 1983; Roberts, Duggan and Noble, 1983). For example, one study of 647 young people in a local labour market showed that West Indians were significantly more likely to be unemployed than were whites or Asians, even after controlling for differences in educational qualifications, parental unemployment, social class and attitudes towards employment (Stafford, Jackson and Banks, 1980). Another study of 166 young males in London and Birmingham showed that "....West Indians are more likely to 'suffer' the consequence sparked off by dismissals and redundancies, and recurrent unemployment is a larger phenomenon for them than it is for similarly educated whites" (Dex, 1983). This latter sample were studied within the period 1971 to 1976, whilst from more recent field-work it is suggested that black unemployment rates (measured as the proportion of time spent unemployed since leaving school) are roughly twice those of whites (Roberts, Duggan and Noble, 1983). However, whilst there is considerable evidence of racial disadvantage, there are also deficiencies in the reported research in terms of sampling and in terms of the level of detail of labour market histories.

For example, Dex (1983) worked with a matched sample of 166 males drawn from London and Birmingham, whilst Stafford et al. (1980) studied a mixed ethnic sample from one labour market. Whilst the labour market histories of Dex's sample were very detailed, covering a five year period, it is uncertain as to how they can be generalised to other areas of the country, and the findings of Stafford et al. are restricted to a cross sectional view of employment status differences.

4. THE PRESENT SAMPLE

The interview schedule at both time one (1982) and time two (1983) included a full history of employment status changes during the preceding year. Nine status categories were used for recording histories: employed full-time, apprenticeship, employed part-time, work experience on employers' premises

35

(WEEP), other YOP schemes, further education, unemployed and actively looking for work, unemployed but not actively looking because it wasn't worth it, and unemployed but not actively looking because of sickness or other plans. For the employed status groups details were recorded of job title, duration and reason for leaving. For YOP status groups the scheme type and duration were recorded. For the unemployed status groups details were taken on duration and whether or not they were registered.

The raw data, consisting of entries in the employment history matrix, were then converted into a number of indices, both continuous and categorical. These included the proportion of time spent unemployed, the number of spells of unemployment, the duration of the current spell, the number of job starts, proportion of time spent in employment, and proportion of time spent on YOP or in further education. In addition each youngster was classified into one of the following groups: continuously unemployed since leaving school, experience of job(s) without YOP, experience of YOP without job(s), experience of both YOP and job(s). And at time two the categories of currently employed and currently on YOP were added.

5. UNEMPLOYMENT DURING THE FIRST TWO YEARS OUT OF SCHOOL

From the self-reported personal histories, three indices of unemployment experience were created: the proportion of time spent unemployed, the number of spells of unemployment and the duration of the current spell of unemployment. Naturally, the latter measure applied only to those unemployed at time two (see Table 5.1 for statistical details of this).

In 1983 the average duration since leaving school was 108 weeks. The first point to note is the extensive periods of unemployment experienced during these first two years out of school. Those who were still unemployed in 1983 had spent 60% of their time since leaving school unemployed, whilst those employed at the time of the 1983 interview had spent half of their previous two years unemployed. Since leaving school the average number of spells of unemployment was three for the employed and 2.6 for the unemployed. Amongst this latter group the average duration of their current unemployment was just over a year.

For all the measures of unemployment, one-way analyses of variance were carried out to test for sex and ethnic differences, separately for the employed and unemployed. So, for example, amongst the employed, white males were tested against black males for an ethnic effect, and black females were tested against black males for a sex effect, and so on through all possible permutations. The results of these tests can be summarised quite concisely. Amongst those Page for

Table 5.1: Labour Market Histories by Sex, Ethnic Group and Status in 1983

| | Black | | | | White | | | | Totals | |
| | Male | | Female | | Male | | Female | | | |
	E	U	E	U	E	U	E	U	E	U
% of time employed	20.06	6.53	18.78	4.85	29.30	13.32	29.81	10.44	27.11	9.58
% time on YOP/FE	24.21	24.48	41.28	30.60	18.45	17.89	18.22	17.66	21.25	21.34
% of time unemployed (Total approx. to 100%)	55.15	68.99	39.89	64.03	50.15	68.72	50.91	71.91	50.34	68.98
No. of jobs	1.15	0.36	1.00	0.32	1.74	0.78	1.86	0.72	1.63	0.59
No. of unemployment spells	3.24	2.59	3.17	2.40	2.91	2.66	3.05	2.74	3.04	2.63
Length of current unemployment in weeks (average)		54.09		46.41		48.27		50.98		51.91
% continuously* unemployed (since 1982)		56.00		35.60		45.20		43.50		45.88
% continuously* unemployed for 2 years (since leaving school)	11.64		17.55		15.64		13.54		13.49	

* Base: unemployed follow-up only (n = 490);
E = Employed in 1983, n = 217; U = Unemployed in 1983, n = 1065

37

employed in 1983 there were no statistically significant sex or ethnic differences in unemployment experiences. That is, within each ethnic group males and females experienced similar percentages of their time unemployed and similar number of spells of unemployment. And within each sex group, blacks and whites also had similar unemployment experiences. Among the currently unemployed, however, the statistical tests showed that white males had a shorter average length of current unemployment (48 weeks) than did black males (54 weeks). In contrast, white females had spent a greater proportion of time unemployed (72%) than black females (64%). The only significant sex difference was the longer length of current unemployment of black males (54 weeks) compared with black females (46 weeks). There were no sex differences amongst the whites.

Two indices of continuous unemployment were also created, one for the period between 1982 and 1983, the other for the total period since leaving school. Sub-group comparisons on these measures are also shown in Table 5.1. Almost half (46%) of those currently unemployed at time two had been so for the whole period since time one. Black males were particularly likely to have been continuously unemployed (56%), compared with 36% for black females, 54% for white males and 43% for white females. Of those currently unemployed 13% had also been continuously unemployed since leaving school. There were no significant sex or ethnic differences in this respect.

6.   INTERMITTENT EMPLOYMENT

The vast majority of the sample had some brief experience of jobs during the two years, and two particular indices of this are also shown in Table 5.1. These are the number of job starts since leaving school and the proportion of time spent in employment. Overall, the proportion of time spent in employment was 27% for the currently employed and 10% for the currently unemployed. Their respective numbers of job starts were 1.63 and 0.59 on average. Within the two status categories there were a number of significant sex and ethnic differences. Employed white males had both a greater proportion of time in employment (29% versus 20%) and a greater number of job starts (1.74 vs. 1.15) than employed black males. Employed white females also had a greater number of job starts than black females. Amongst the currently unemployed, white males also had both a greater proportion of time employed and a greater number of job starts than black males. Similarly for unemployed white females as compared with black females. There were no significant sex differences at all in these measures of employment experiences.

38

7.   THE YOUTH OPPORTUNITIES PROGRAMME

Both the currently employed and the currently unemployed had spent 21% of their past two years on the Youth Opportunities Programme or in further education (see Table 5.1). In effect most of this experience was in YOP. Within these two status groups there were some significant sex and ethnic group differences. Employed black females had spent a greater proportion of time on YOP/FE (41%) than both white females (18%) and black males (24%). There were no sex differences among employed whites. Amongst the currently unemployed, white males had spent a smaller proportion of time on YOP/FE than had black males. The only sex difference was between black males and females, with the latter having spent the greater proportion of time on YOP/FE.

8.   TYPES OF EARLY CAREER

For the core longitudinal sample, employment histories at time one and time two have been combined into an overall categorisation of labour market experiences during the first two years out of school. The resulting six status categories are shown in Table 5.2. (These results exclude the boost sample.)

Those currently employed (n = 174) and on YOP/FE (n = 43) at time two are shown as separate categories, whilst the unemployed at time two are subdivided into four groups. These are the continuously unemployed (n = 87), those who have had job(s) but no YOP (n = 69), those who have had YOP but no job (n = 236), and those who have had both job(s) and YOP (n = 123).

This categorisation, by sex and ethnic group, is also shown in Table 5.2. Overall there were no sex differences of statistical significance. Although there was a slightly greater proportion of females continuously unemployed (14% compared with 11% of males) this difference was not statistically significant. In contrast, the picture in respect of ethnic differences is more complex with significant differences between the sub-groups apparent throughout the two year period. There was a clearly marked trend for blacks to be less likely to have had a job and more likely to have been on YOP. For example, a greater proportion of whites were currently employed at time two (28% of white males and of white females, compared with 14% of black males and 16% of black females). Similarly, of those currently unemployed at time two, 31% of white males and 28% of white females had held at least one job, compared with 19% of black males and 18% of black females.

Table 5.2: Labour Market History During First Two Years Out of School (adding t1 and t2) by Sex and Ethnic Group (row percents in brackets)

| | Currently Employed | Currently on YOP | Continuous Unemployment | Currently Unemployed | | |
				Job(s), No YOP	YOP, No Job	JOP and Jobs(s)
Males:						
Black	21 (13.9)	15 (9.9)	16 (10.6)	9 (6.0)	71 (47.0)	19 (12.6)
White	72 (27.8)	11 (4.2)	27 (10.4)	30 (11.6)	68 (26.3)	51 (19.7)
Females:						
Black	12 (16.4)	6 (8.2)	9 (12.3)	3 (4.1)	33 (45.2)	10 (13.7)
White	69 (27.7)	11 (4.4)	35 (14.1)	27 (10.8)	64 (25.7)	43 (17.3)
TOTALS	174	43	87	69	236	123

9.   CONTINUITY BETWEEN YEAR ONE AND YEAR TWO EXPERIENCES

The relationships between year one and year two experiences in terms of proportions of time in each status are shown in Table 5.3. These data refer to the core longitudinal sample for whom personal histories at time one and time two are available, thus excluding the boost sample. In Table 5.3 no distinction is made in employment status at time two, but the proportions are presented separately for the sex and ethnic sub-groups.

In the case of black males there is no significant difference between year one and year two in the proportion of time spent employed. There is, however, a significant fall (p <0.001) from 29% to 13% in the proportion of time spent on YOP or in further education. This fall then accounts for the substantial increase from 64% to 78% in the proportion of time spent unemployed. In contrast a different pattern emerges amongst black females, who experience a considerable increase (p <0.001) from 2% to 12% in the proportion of time employed. This increase is accounted for almost equally by a reduction in the proportion of time spent in YOP/FE and unemployment. White males and white females display similar patterns of labour market experiences. Both groups increase significantly (p <0.01) the proportion of time employed, from around 12% to around 18%. At the same time the proportion of time on YOP/FE falls significantly (p <0.001). For males the change is from 25% to 8%, and for females from 23% to 7%. This fall accounts for some of the increase in employment, but also for a significant increase (p <0.001) in the proportion of time unemployed. For males this goes up from 63% to 73%, and for females from 65% to 74%.

These same proportion variables are also analysed separately for the employed and the unemployed at time two (see Table 5.4 and 5.5). As might be expected there are different patterns for the two status groups. The unemployed at time two show a significant decrease (p <0.01, black males and white females) or no change (black females and white males) in the proportion of time employed. All except black females show a significant fall (p <0.001) in proportion of time on YOP/FE. And similarly all except black females experience a significant increase (p <0.001) in the proportion of their time unemployed.

In contrast, those employed at time two all show significant increases in the proportion of time employed, and significant decreases in the proportion of time unemployed. Both white groups also show a significant fall in proportion of time on YOP/FE.

Table 5.6 shows an analysis of time one histories against time two histories. This table is of interest since it tells us something of the changes that occurred in the experiences of this young sample. First, let us take the prediction of

41

Table 5.3: Comparison of Labour Market Experience Between the First Year and the Second Year Out of School (Follow-up Sample)

| | Blacks | | | | Whites | | | |
| | Males (n = 150) | | Females (n = 73) | | Males (n = 259) | | Females (n = 246) | |
Proportion of time ...	t1	t2	t1	t2	t1	t2	t1	t2
Employed	7.22 (15.45)	8.49 (23.19)	1.86 (6.80)	12.01*** (25.95)	12.29 (21.83)	18.07** (29.36)	11.64 (21.63)	17.69** (28.84)
On YOP/FE	29.22 (26.02)	13.30*** (24.66)	30.97 (29.87)	24.52 (35.27)	24.51 (28.14)	7.58*** (19.12)	22.97 (26.24)	7.39*** (18.61)
Unemployed	63.56 (27.55)	78.00*** (31.19)	67.16 (30.54)	62.10 (38.06)	62.82 (30.14)	72.82*** (34.40)	64.58 (28.77)	73.97*** (33.37)

Notes:

(i)   Figures are column percentages, standard deviations in brackets.

(ii) Column totals approximate to 100% in some cases because of rounding errors.

(iii) In this table time spent in further education is merged with time spent on the Youth Opportunities Programme. For the present purpose it does not seem necessary to disaggregate these categories, especially so since FE accounts for only a small proportion of time. For example, in the first year it accounted for 3.36% of the time.

(iv) t1 refers to activities during the first year out of school, and t2 refers to activities during the second year out of school.

(v)   Significance of change from t1 to t2: *** indicates p <0.001; ** indicates p <0.01.

42

Table 5.4: Comparison of Labour Market Experience Between the First Year and the Second Year for the Unemployed at Time Two

Proportion of time ...	Blacks				Whites			
	Males (n = 114)		Females (n = 55)		Males (n = 176)		Females (n = 168)	
	t1	t2	t1	t2	t1	t2	t1	t2
Employed	5.13 (11.62)	1.56** (8.70)	2.11 (7.54)	3.66 (11.85)	10.06 (19.25)	6.89 (18.59)	9.04 (18.41)	4.34** (11.72)
On YOP/FE	30.90 (26.67)	10.68*** (23.22)	25.38 (26.78)	21.61 (32.99)	23.76 (26.56)	5.49*** (15.79)	22.82 (26.16)	5.63*** (16.14)
Unemployed	63.97 (26.80)	87.76*** (24.24)	72.51 (28.01)	72.92 (35.00)	65.61 (29.37)	87.19*** (24.69)	68.14 (27.70)	89.08*** (21.94)

For explanatory notes see Table 5.3, p.42.

Table 5.5: Comparison of Labour Market Experience Between the First Year and the Second Year for the Employed at Time Two

| | Blacks | | | | Whites | | | |
| | Males (n = 36) | | Females (n = 18) | | Males (n = 83) | | Females (n = 80) | |
Proportion of time ...	t1	t2	t1	t2	t1	t2	t1	t2
Employed	13.82 (22.84)	30.42* (37.34)	1.10 (3.77)	37.51*** (38.61)	17.02 (25.98)	41.78*** (33.73)	16.79 (26.38)	45.27*** (33.87)
On YOP/FE	23.93 (23.42)	21.60 (27.50)	48.06 (33.02)	33.43 (41.24)	26.10 (31.33)	12.02** (24.26)	23.65 (27.00)	10.89** (22.48)
Unemployed	62.25 (30.18)	47.10* (30.85)	50.84 (32.91)	29.05* (26.65)	56.89 (31.06)	42.31** (32.19)	57.05 (29.93)	40.38*** (30.77)

For explanatory notes see Table 5.3, p.42.

44

Table 5.6: Labour Market History During the First Year (to t1) and During the Second Year (between t1 and t2) Since Leaving School (row percents in brackets)

	Labour Market History at t2 Currently Unemployed					
	Currently Employed	Continuous Unemployment	Job(s), No YOP	YOP, No Job	YOP and Job(s)	Totals
Continuous unemployment	24 (16.0)	87 (58.0)	8 (5.3)	28 (18.7)	3 (2.0)	150
Labour market history up to t1:						
Job(s), no YOP	42 (36.8)	48 (42.1)	13 (11.4)	10 (8.8)	1 (0.9)	114
YOP, no job	73 (21.3)	168 (48.0)	32 (9.1)	69 (19.7)	8 (2.3)	350
YOP and job(s)	34 (29.3)	50 (43.1)	13 (11.2)	14 (12.1)	5 (4.3)	116
Totals	173	353	66	121	17	730

Note: Due to missing data two respondents could not be coded by this classification.

45

employment status at time two from the histories at time one. The 173 who were employed at time two represent almost a quarter of those re-interviewed. This group was composed of 24 who were continuously unemployed at time one, 42 who had held a job but not been on YOP, 73 who had been on YOP but not had a job, and 34 who had both held a job and been on YOP. Recall that they were all unemployed at time one. To assess whether the employed at time two were more likely to come from any particular group at time one we need to express these numbers as proportions of their original time one groups. In descending order, then, the most likely group to be employed at time two were those who had held a job in their first year but had not been on YOP (37% of this group were employed at time two,) followed by those who had experience of YOP and employment (29%), those who had been on YOP but had not had a job (21%), and finally those who had been continuously unemployed at time one (16%).

Second, it is of interest to see which groups were more likely to be continuously unemployed during their second year, using a similar line of argument as above. Approximately half of the sample were unemployed continuously between times one and two, made up of, in descending order, those continuously unemployed at time one (58%), those with experience of YOP but not employment (48%), those with experience of YOP and jobs (43%), and those with experience of employment but not YOP (42%). It would seem from these data then that there is some consistency in the histories, in that getting off to a bad start in the first year leads to a greater likelihood of extensive unemployment in the second year.

Those who had experience of YOP during their second year were more likely to be drawn from the groups who either had continuous unemployment in the first year or who were also on YOP during that year. Thus, only a small proportion of those who had not been on YOP in the first year were likely to do so during the second year.

10. THE EXPERIENCE OF THIS SAMPLE IN CONTEXT

Recent analysis of the Labour Force Survey (Barber, 1985) showed that in the 16 to 24 age group around 40% of West Indian and "other minority" males (excluding Asian) were unemployed, compared to almost 20% of white males. The equivalent percentages for females were 25% of West Indians and 15% of whites. Reports beginning to appear in the late 1970s suggested that, while increasing numbers of young people were affected by unemployment, continuous spells were still relatively short (Daniel and Stilgoe, 1977). From the experiences of our sample in the 1980s, however, we can see most clearly that those young people most at risk are experiencing substantial unemployment, both as aggregated short spells and also as long, continuous spells of uninterrupted joblessness.

One study concluded that while local youth unemployment levels remain below 25% only small minorities of 'young people with problems' descend into serious predicaments (Roberts, Noble and Duggan, 1982a and b). These 'young people with problems' may be poor interviewees, repeatedly rejected applicants, suffer acute shyness, offend employers with 'way-out' manner or appearances, or possess serious criminal records. Whilst remedies for such problems may not be immediately available, it is clear that many other youngsters without such problems have also descended into serious predicaments.

The present study can also be put in context by comparison with some statistics from the recently mounted National Youth Cohort Study. This is a large representative survey carried out in Summer 1985, about a year after the sample became eligible to leave school. Around 9% of the sample were registered unemployed during the first year out of school (1% unregistered). Needless to say this 9% are not the same group throughout the year. Comparative figures for the other major status categories at age 17 were roughly a quarter on YTS, another quarter in full-time employment and 40% in full-time education (Jones, Gray and Clough, 1987). The National Youth Cohort Study therefore shows that while YTS may have removed many 16 year olds from the unemployment register, there is nonetheless around 10% of 16-17 year olds still experiencing unemployment. The results of the study reported here are just as relevant to this 10% as they are to the age cohorts from which our sample was selected.

It might seem appropriate at this point to ask the question of why some of our sample were more successful than others in finding jobs. There are many factors that could be listed as potential predictors of success. For example, having a more positive attitude, or living in the South of England. This question was investigated in a very thorough way through the use of a wide range of variables. Consequently the nature of these variables needs describing fully and so the question is returned to later in Chapter 7.

11. SUMMARY

This chapter has examined the early careers of the sample during the first two years after school-leaving in terms of a range of indices of unemployment, employment, youth training and further education. For both the unemployed and employed in 1983 there had been extensive periods of unemployment, 69% and 50% of their time respectively. The average current duration of unemployment was just over a year for the currently unemployed, amongst whom 13% had been continuously unemployed since school. Amongst the unemployed in 1983 white males had a significantly shorter duration of current unemployment than black males, and white females spent a greater proportion of their time unemployed than black females. Black males also had longer current spells of unemployment than black females.

Overall, the proportion of time spent in employment was 17% for the currently employed and 10% for the currently unemployed. Amongst the currently employed, black males were significantly more disadvantaged in this respect than white males, although there was no ethnic difference among females. Amongst the unemployed the ethnic disadvantage was significant for both males and females. There were no sex differences in employment experiences.

The proportion of time spent on YOP or in Further Education was 21% for both the employed and unemployed in 1983. Employed black females had significantly more experience of YOP/FE than both white females and black males. Amongst the unemployed, black males had significantly more YOP/FE experience than white males, but less than black females.

Taking the labour market experience as a whole there was a clearly marked indication that blacks were less likely to be employed after two years in the labour market and less likely to have had a job at all during that time. At the same time blacks participated in more YOP/FE and thus the unemployment indices alone do not reveal the extent of their disadvantage. Although there were some sex differences on individual labour market indices there was no overall clearly identified trend. Comparisons of the first year out of school with the second year suggested that there was a close correspondence in labour market experiences, such that those who got off to a bad start continued to fare badly. Combined with this we see a minority of the sample emerging as the long-term unemployed.

Chapter 6

UNEMPLOYMENT, PSYCHOLOGICAL WELL-BEING AND PERSONALITY

1.   A REVIEW OF THE LITERATURE

This chapter considers the effect that unemployment might have upon psychological well-being, personality and identity development. The research literature on these topics is underpinned with the theoretical notion that unemployment is an undesirable state which results in maladjustments of various kinds. This is not an unreasonable assumption, based upon earlier work on unemployment in the 1930s (Eisenberg and Lazarsfeld, 1938, and summarised in Jahoda, 1979, 1982). But what conclusions are to be drawn from more recent research into youth unemployment? Before presenting our own research findings we first review the recent literature in greater detail than was possible in Chapter 3, using the following seven headings:

   1.1   General psychological distress
   1.2   Depression and depressive affect
   1.3   Anxiety
   1.4   Self-esteem
   1.5   Happiness, life satisfaction
   1.6   Psycho-social development
   1.7   Mood states

Within each category a distinction is made where appropriate between cross-sectional studies with comparison groups, cross-sectional studies without comparison groups, longitudinal studies, and studies of unemployment duration.

1.1 General Psychological Distress

A widely used measure of general psychological distress is the General Health Questionnaire (GHQ) (Goldberg, 1972, 1978, 1981), a self-administered screening test for detecting non-psychotic psychiatric disorder. The GHQ has been subject to considerable validation studies (e.g. as reported in Goldberg,

1978 and Henderson, Duncan-Jones, Byrne, Scott and Adcock, 1979) in which it has been shown to correlate highly with more extensive clinical interviews. Of importance here is the finding of high validity among a young community sample (Banks, 1983).

Papers reporting the effects or concomitants of youth unemployment on GHQ scores are quite wide-ranging, both in methodology and in location of the fieldwork. In order to better understand these findings the conclusions are ordered into four categories: cross-sectional studies, longitudinal studies, studies of the effect of unemployment duration, and studies looking at variables which moderate the relationship between unemployment and GHQ scores.

A number of papers have appeared in the literature reporting cross-sectional GHQ data for unemployed young people and an equivalent comparison group of employed young people. Most of these arise from one particular study of two age cohorts in the city of Leeds (Banks, Clegg, Jackson, Kemp, Stafford and Wall, 1980; Stafford, Jackson and Banks, 1980; Stafford, 1982; Banks and Jackson, 1982; Jackson, Stafford, Banks and Warr, 1983; Banks, Mullings and Jackson, 1983). Although these papers are quite diverse because they test different hypotheses, the conclusion in respect of cross-sectional comparisons between unemployed and employed can be stated quite simply. There is an unequivocal connection between GHQ and current employment status, with the unemployed of both sexes scoring higher on the GHQ (and thereby reporting greater distress). Typically the mean scale scores on the GHQ-12 for the employed were between 7 and 9, compared with 12 to 15 among the unemployed.

Two other studies also report highly significant differences between the GHQ scores of the employed and the unemployed (Donovan and Oddy, 1982; Oddy, Donovan and Pardoe, 1984). For example, using the GHQ-30, the mean scores for unemployed males and females were 24.83 and 34.08 respectively, in contrast to 14.00 and 19.50 for employed males and females (Donovan and Oddy, 1982).

A number of studies have focussed exclusively on groups of unemployed youth without including a comparison group of employed young people. This is not necessarily a criticism since the objectives have often been to investigate sub-group differences (e.g. sex, ethnicity) or to test for the effect of moderating variables. Furthermore, comparisons can be made with other studies using the same dependent variable.

Finlay-Jones and Eckhardt (1981, 1984) combined the use of the GHQ-30 with the Present State Examination in a study of 401 single 16-24 year old Australians. The GHQ-30 identified 56% as probable cases, and by linking GHQ scores to PSE data on a sub-sample of 75 the proportion with severe psychiatric disorder was estimated to be 49%. In 70% of cases the onset of their disorder followed unemployment, and in more than half of these there was no evidence of any other recent stress apart from unemployment. By comparing their results with those of a previous study of employed 15-25 year olds in the same city, Finlay-Jones and Eckhardt estimate that unemployment in this age group raised the odds of having a psychiatric disorder by a factor of six.

Two papers report data from the first stage of our present study, on 1150 unemployed 17 year olds from 11 urban areas in England (Warr, Banks and Ullah, 1985; Ullah, Banks and Warr, 1985). The mean GHQ-12 scale score was 11.88, which was statistically significantly higher than equivalent employed samples. As in the Finlay-Jones and Eckhardt study, this study also reported that psychological symptoms usually commenced after the onset of unemployment. Two other cross-sectional studies have used an alternative measure, the Langner 22-item scale of psychological distress (Langner, 1962). Furnham (1983) identified differences on the Langner scale according to employment status, with the unemployed scoring higher. However, this sample was of all ages (with 50 individuals under 21 years old) and it is impossible to conclude from the paper whether this finding applied equally to all age groups. Halford and Learner (1984) used the Langner scale on 126 males and females (average age = 18 years) attending Commonwealth Youth Support Scheme centres in Australia. Although there were no direct comparison groups in this study the authors conclude that their sample of unemployed young people had a high rate of mental health problems, and were therefore coping poorly.

An important question arises from the previously reported studies as to whether the cross-sectional differences in well-being occur as a result of unemployment or because of prior differences within the samples before entering the labour market. For example, it may be that the experience of psychological distress before leaving school impairs a young person's chances of securing employment. This question of causality has been addressed in one longitudinal study reported in the literature (Banks and Jackson, 1982). This paper contains a comprehensive analysis of two age cohorts, one of which was tested whilst at school and then subsequently on two occasions up to two years out of school. The clear conclusion was that the experience of unemployment was more likely to lead to general distress, rather than the reverse. No significant differences in GHQ between those who were subsequently unemployed and those who were subsequently employed were observed whilst the cohort was at school, but significantly different scores between the employed and the unemployed were obtained at subsequent interview points.

Five recent studies have investigated whether increasing duration of unemployment is associated with greater psychological distress as assessed by the GHQ. Warr, Jackson and Banks (1982) used both correlational analysis and analysis of variance to detect possible non-linear trends in the relationship between GHQ-12 and durations of between 10 and 23 weeks of continuous unemployment. Amongst males there was no relationship between GHQ and duration of unemployment, even after partialling out the moderating effect of employment commitment. Amongst females, however, there was a significant negative relation between duration and GHQ, so that longer spells of unemployment were associated with lower distress scores. The authors explain this sex difference by a greater withdrawal from the labour market on the part of young women. That is, a large proportion had ceased to look for work because they were either expecting a baby or were caring for a young child.

A subsequent study, again using the GHQ-12, produced findings which suggested a curvilinear relationship based upon three duration categories: up to 3 weeks, 4 to 9 weeks, and greater than 9 weeks (Breakwell, Harrison and Propper, 1984) Results showed that, for both males and females, the 4-9 week category suffered greater distress than the other two groups. This finding was explained by the authors as reflecting the uncertainty of whether or not these young people would obtain a youth training (YOP) place. At the time there was a requirement for unemployed youth to wait six weeks before being eligible for a training place. This explanation remains speculative though, since no empirical data was reported as to how the young people viewed their future prospects.

Two other studies investigating the duration hypothesis failed to find support for the relationship. Finlay-Jones and Eckhardt (1984) searched for a relationship between the GHQ-30 and unemployment durations of between two weeks and five years (mean = 10 months). They reported no significant association, but from the published data it is not possible to see whether a linear or non-linear model was used. That is, it was not clear whether GHQ scores were expected to increase progressively with longer duration, or whether, say, GHQ scores were expected to be higher in the medium duration categories and lower in the short and very long duration categories. Jackson and Warr (1984), in their large survey of all ages of unemployed men, include the 16-19 year age group in their analyses. Even after controlling for a range of moderating variables (such as employment commitment, job-seeking, and income change) they failed to find a relationship between the GHQ and durations of unemployment of from less than one month up to greater than 12 months among the 16-19 age group.

Analysis of the first stage of our present study also found no relationship between GHQ-12 and length of time unemployed (up to one year) (Warr, Banks and Ullah, 1985).

The few papers that have reported on the duration hypothesis have covered, collectively, quite a wide range of unemployment durations, and the conclusion to be drawn from them is that unemployment duration by itself is not associated with general psychological distress among young people. The research literature does not adequately explain why this is so, but two features stand out. First, it is highly likely that duration acts as a 'carrier' variable, in the sense that it is associated with certain situational and developmental trends. The findings of Warr et al. (1982) and Breakwell et al. (1984) support this view. Second, GHQ, as the dependent variable, may cause interpretative problems because of its response scale, which asks for recent changes compared with some time ago, or with 'the usual situation'. Because cross-sectional studies, as reported in this section, necessarily use retrospective unemployment duration as the independent variable, it may be that like is not being compared with like. For example, respondents with a recent short spell of unemployment may be comparing their current psychological state with that of some time ago when they were possibly employed. In contrast, those with, say, a 12 months spell of current unemployment will probably be comparing the present with their psychological state whilst unemployed at an earlier point in time. Such a design as typically used in the studies reported here is unlikely to disentangle this methodological problem. Clearly a longitudinal study, if carefully designed by controlling for employment status and labour market history at different interview points, would go some way towards solving this problem.

1.2 Depression and Depressive Affect

Several studies have used different measures of depression or depressive affect as outcome measures of school-leaver unemployment, with comparison groups of young people in employment, in further education, in youth training or still at school. Two papers report the use of the Leeds Depression scale on different samples (Donovan and Oddy, 1982; Oddy, Donovan and Pardoe, 1984). Both studies showed that the unemployed were significantly more depressed than the employed, and the later study also showed that they were more depressed than those on YOP schemes.

Three Australian studies have examined the association between depression and unemployment status. Patton and Noller (1984), using the Beck Depression Inventory, identified significantly greater depression in a small sample (n = 21) of unemployed young people, compared to those in employment or still at school. Tiggemann and Winefield (1980), from another study (n = 118), failed to find cross-sectional differences between the employed and unemployed on both a single item depressed mood measure and on six items from the Zung Depression Scale (Zung, 1965). Winefield and Tiggemann (1985) used both the Rosenberg six-item scale to measure depressive affect and a single item depressed mood measure. In both

53

cases the unemployed were significantly more depressed than those in employment, in Further Education and those still at school.

A further study using the Beck Depression Inventory, on a small sample, showed that those in employment were significantly less depressed than those unemployed or on YOP (Branthwaite and Garcia, 1985).

The general conclusion to be drawn from these studies is that unemployed youth exhibit greater depression than employed youth, although there is some ambiguity about contrasts with youth in training. This latter issue is returned to later, as are the other studies using depression as an outcome but without comparison groups (e.g. Feather and Davenport, 1981; Feather and Barber, 1983; Warr, Banks and Ullah, 1985).

Most of the papers previously cited in this section also report longitudinal data. Tiggemann and Winefield (1980), although failing to find cross-sectional differences, did note that the unemployed had become significantly more depressed six months after leaving school. As possible reasons for the lack of cross-sectional difference they mention the short time interval (six months) between t1 and t2, and the fact that many recent school leavers regard the first few months as a 'holiday'. Two more recent papers by the same authors report on a larger longitudinal study of young Australians before and after leaving school (Tiggemann and Winefield, 1984; Winefield and Tiggemann, 1985). The earlier paper includes a longitudinal analysis with an eight month interval between school leaving and follow-up, whilst the second paper covers the interval of two years between observations. In both sets of analyses depressed mood (a single item measure) was shown to be a predisposing factor in determining whether or not a person was unemployed at the second interview; in the later paper this measure was simultaneously identified as an effect or consequence of becoming unemployed. Also in both analyses depressive affect (6-item measure) was identified as a consequence of unemployment but not a predisposing factor. Another Australian longitudinal study to look at depression, in this case using the Beck Depression Inventory, was that of Patton and Noller (1984). They found that the unemployed had significantly greater depression than the employed, and that the two groups did not previously differ on this measure, concluding that unemployment was causally implicated in this change. A final longitudinal study to have measured depression, in this case using the Leeds Depression Scale, was that of Oddy, Donovan and Pardoe (1984). Although they state that the unemployed were more likely to be depressed, no data on longitudinal change has yet been reported from this study.

In respect of possible relationships between unemployment duration and the measures of depression the clear conclusion is that there is no evidence available to suggest such relationships. This conclusion is based upon the findings of three papers. Feather and Davenport (1981) used a one item measure of depressed affect ("When you think about being unemployed, how does it make you feel?") against a mean duration of 30.59 weeks. Feather and Barber (1983) used the Beck Depression Inventory against quite wide-ranging durations with a mean of 57.51 weeks. And Warr, Banks and Ullah (1985) used an abbreviated form of the Zung Depression Scale against durations of up to a year with a mean of 26.31 weeks. All three papers report that outcome measures of depression were independent of length of unemployment.

1.3 Anxiety

Only a few studies have used anxiety as a measure of psychological well-being in unemployment research. Donovan and Oddy (1982) identified greater anxiety, as measured by the Leeds Anxiety Scale (Snaith, Bridge and Hamilton, 1976), among a small sample of unemployed school-leavers, when compared with a matched group of employed school-leavers. The same anxiety scale was also used in a later, prospective, study with the conclusion that 'the unemployed leavers were distinctly more likely to be ... anxious ...!' However, no data is reported in this paper.

Cross-sectional results from the present study have been reported, in which a short form of the Zung Anxiety scale was used (Warr, Banks and Ullah, 1985; Ullah, Banks and Warr, 1985). This study had no employed comparison group although its importance lies in the differential effects of unemployment within the sample. It will therefore be returned to later. On the whole, therefore, there is hardly any research evidence linking anxiety to unemployment.

1.4 Self-esteem

Most research into youth unemployment and self-esteem has used the Rosenberg scale (Rosenberg, 1965) or some adaptation of it (e.g. O'Malley and Bachman, 1979). One paper reported results on two items ('satisfied with yourself' and 'worthwhile as an individual') that are quite similar to items in the Rosenberg scale (Tiggemann and Winefield, 1980). This study showed that the unemployed had become less satisfied with themselves since leaving school, but did not consider themselves less worthwhile as individuals. Other studies, using multi-item measures, also produce conflicting evidence, largely over whether it is the employed or the unemployed who change and over whether males and females are affected similarly. Donovan and Oddy (1982) also report significant cross-sectional differences between the employed and the unemployed. Gurney (1980b) showed that only among females was there a significant contrast in self-esteem between the unemployed and the employed, with there being no difference between the unemployed and the school-returners. More importantly, Gurney's findings showed that the unemployed did not show any longitudinal decline in self-esteem from when they were at school. Similarly, Tiggemann and Winefield (1984) showed that it was the employed who gained in self-esteem, whereas the unemployed showed no change. In contrast, Patton and Noller (1984) produced contrary findings, that unemployment did have an adverse impact on self-esteem, which also decreased with increasing duration of unemployment.

This line of research was taken a step further by Warr and Jackson (1983), who differentiated between negative and positive self-esteem within the adapted Rosenberg scale. They showed no difference between the unemployed and the employed in positive self-esteem, but a significant difference was found in negative self-esteem. The unemployed regarded themselves in a more negative light. This difference applied equally to males and females, and resulted from the unemployment experience rather than as a result of prior differences within the sample.

1.5 Happiness, Life Satisfaction

Two British studies have reported lower life satisfaction amongst the unemployed compared to the employed recent school-leaver (Gaskell and Smith, 1981; Donovan and Oddy, 1982). And in two Australian studies the unemployed reported less happiness, which was determined through longitudinal analyses to be a consequence of unemployment experiences (Tiggemann and Winefield, 1980; Tiggemann and Winefield, 1984; Winefield and Tiggemann, 1985).

1.6 Identity and Psycho-social Development

A number of papers have appeared reporting results from an Australian longitudinal study of school-leavers (Gurney 1980a and b, 1981). One interesting aim of this study was to apply the developmental theory of Erikson (1968), of which adolescent identity resolution forms a focal point. Despite studying only short durations of unemployment the conclusion was drawn that "unemployment has the effect of inhibiting development in school-leavers, rather than of inflicting trauma as is sometimes popularly supposed" (Gurney, 1980a). There was in addition a somewhat speculative conclusion that in girls the experience of moving into employment provides a special boost (i.e. the effect is more marked than in boys) to identity development and maturity.

1.7 Mood States (Other Than Above)

Several studies have also looked at mood states other than those such as depression, anxiety, happiness and satisfaction, which have been dealt with previously. Such moods states, typically investigated by bipolar scales, include 'bored', 'lonely', 'angry with self', 'angry with society', 'helpless', and so on.

These studies appear to be exclusively Australian in origin. Turtle, Cranfield, Rogers, Reuman and Williams (1978), in a survey of 150 young people aged between 16 and 26 years, found that the unemployed were becoming more withdrawn and despondent, and they experienced feelings of discontent, boredom, frustration and loneliness. In a report on 12 clinical case studies Kosky (1980) noted the unemployed "start their search for employment on leaving school with confidence and optimism. As successive attempts to find a job proved fruitless, they got angry. They reckoned they had been deceived by school and when their friends found work they felt unfairly treated ... Suddenly they felt let down - powerless to do anything about their situation, impotent in the face of seemingly endless rejections of their offered services" (Kosky, 1980, p.845-6). Tiggemann and Winefield (1980) identified the young unemployed as more lonely than the employed as a result of their unemployment. In a later study the same authors added increased boredom to the list of mood states created by unemployment, and amongst girls, increased helplessness (Tiggemann and Winefield, 1984). This latter study concluded that greater anger with society and loneliness were present at school and could be regarded as predisposing factors to unemployment. A later publication amended the preliminary conclusions, so that loneliness was seen as a predisposing factor only in males, whilst anger (internally and externally oriented) and helplessness were seen as consequences of unemployment (Winefield and Tiggemann, 1985).

2.   RESULTS FROM THE PRESENT STUDY

This next section focusses on the relationship between unemployment experiences among our sample and a group of psychological outcome variables. These variables are general psychological distress, depression, anxiety, concern about and stigma from unemployment, and two dimensions of personality - achievement orientation and sociability. There are two primary objectives:

(i)   First, to assess whether young people who experienced longer periods of unemployment were also reporting to us lower levels of psychological well-being, and more concern about and stigma from unemployment. This objective bears directly on the much discussed phase models of psychological responses to unemployment (e.g. Eisenberg and Lazarsfeld, 1938; Harrison, 1976; Hill, 1978).

(ii) Second, to determine whether there was any longitudinal change in psychological well-being and personality between the two interviews. For those who were in jobs when interviewed in 1983 we would predict a marked improvement in well-being compared with those remaining unemployed.

Before describing the results we need to say briefly how the outcome variables were measured.

General psychological distress: The 12-item version of the General Health Questionnaire was used, because it is brief, easy to administer, and has high validity and internal reliability (Banks et al., 1980; Banks, 1983). Respondents are asked to compare themselves in the past few weeks with how they have felt in the past few years. Items cover anxiety, depression, low self-esteem and day-to-day difficulties. For example, to the question 'Have you recently lost much sleep over worry?' the answers 'not at all', 'no more than usual', 'rather more than usual', 'much more than usual' were scored from 0 to 3 respectively. Note that a high score indicates greater ill-health. The mean item score in 1983 was 0.96 for the unemployed and 0.58 for the employed.

The standard administration of the GHQ was followed by specific attention to any symptoms deemed by the scale's originator to be potentially indicative of psychiatric caseness, that is responses scored as 2 or 3 (for example, 'rather more than usual' and 'much more than usual'). For all such symptoms interviewers asked when that change was first noticed and what the respondent believed caused the change.

Depression: A six-item measure of depressed mood was drawn from the 20-item depression scale created for use in clinical research by Zung (1965, 1974). Warr and Parry (1982) have reported substantial validity for this reduced measure in relation to psychiatric diagnosis. Questions cover feelings of worthlessness and unhappiness (for example, 'I feel downhearted and blue'), and responses are on a four-point scale (none or a little of the time, some of the time, a good part of the time, and most or all of the time), scored 0 to 3 such that a high score indicates greater depression. In 1983 the mean item score was 1.18 for the unemployed and 0.64 for the employed.

Anxiety: A six-item scale was derived from Zung's (1974) measure of anxiety. An illustrative item is 'I feel like I'm falling apart and going to pieces'. Responses and scoring were as for the depression measure. The mean item score in 1983 was 0.76 for the unemployed and 0.44 for the employed and coefficient alpha was 0.74. The depression and anxiety scales were intercorrelated 0.53 and were correlated 0.57 and 0.63 respectively with the GHQ measure of general distress, at time one. At time two correlations were very similar.

Concern over unemployment: In order to obtain a measure of affect directly associated with their lack of a job, respondents were asked 'How much does it trouble you that you're unemployed?' Responses (0 to 3) were: it doesn't trouble me at all, it troubles me a bit, it troubles me a lot, and it troubles me a great deal.

Stigma from unemployment: The preceding question was set into a social context by the item: 'How much does it trouble you that other people know you're unemployed?' Responses and scoring were as for the earlier item.

Personality: Two dimensions of personality (sociability and achievement orientation) were assessed using new combinations of short items derived from well-established personality measures (California Psychological Inventory, Gough, 1957; Eysenck Personality Inventory, Eysenck, 1953). The seven items constituting the sociability dimension were: friendly, enjoy meeting new people, enjoy parties, find it easy to talk to people, enjoy telling jokes, sociable, enjoy mixing with people. The seven items constituting the achievement orientation dimension were: determined, like getting things done, keep trying at things, ambitious, like to keep busy, like to plan ahead, can get things organised. Respondents were asked whether each item applied to themselves and the response scale for all items was yes (2), no (0), don't know (1). The substantive results are now organised around the twin objectives that were described earlier.

2.1 The Effect of Unemployment Duration

The idea that with increasingly longer spells of unemployment young people will suffer progressively more symptoms of personal distress arises for two main reasons. First, although based on shaky empirical evidence, the phase model has been given much credence in the literature on psychological responses to unemployment. This model specifically addresses the question of change in psychological outlook with increasing duration of unemployment, and, put at its simplest, suggests the four stages of shock, optimism, pessimism and resignation. Quite clearly, these stages represent substantially different kinds of qualitative experience, not just more or less of the same subjective experience. A rigorous test of the model would therefore be made extremely difficult in a large-scale interview survey in which a high degree of standardisation of measurement is called for. Nonetheless, some insight into whether a phase model of some kind applies to young people's experience is offered from the present study. A second reason is less articulated in the literature but no less pervasive since it is closer to common-sense reasoning. It is, namely, that as a spell of unemployment lengthens and the prospects of escaping from the condition become bleaker, it would be surprising if this process was not reflected in increasing gloom, despondency and general psychological distress.

When interviewed in 1983 the unemployed (n = 1062) were at different stages of their experience of unemployment, varying from having just become unemployed for the second or third time to having been continuously unemployed for two and a half years. A straightforward test of the effect of duration on psychological well-being can therefore be carried out, by calculating the correlation coefficient between unemployment duration and each of the well-being variables. The results can be summarized quite precisely. Neither the GHQ, Zung Depression Scale nor Zung Anxiety Scale were significantly correlated with duration of unemployment. In case there was a non-linear relationship, which could not be detected by the correlation method, the duration variable was split into six categories and analysis of variance was carried out, also controlling for possible sex and ethnic group effects. Again, however, the results were crystal clear. There was no association between duration of unemployment and level of general psychological distress, depression or anxiety.

On turning to the concern expressed by young people about their own unemployment we did find a link between this variable and duration of unemployment, but in a direction which at first seemed counter-intuitive. Table 6.1 shows the relevant data on this question. A one-way analysis of variance for all unemployed (data on the bottom line of Table 6.1) revealed statistically significant relationships between concern and duration of unemployment (p <0.01). Subsequent pairwise comparisons of the six duration categories indicated that the significant contrast was between the shortest duration and longest duration. Concern was thus greatest in the early stages of unemployment, followed by a steady decline until the longest duration where there was a significant fall in concern. Further analysis amongst blacks and whites separately, controlling for sex, revealed that the effect of duration was significant amongst whites, equally for males and females, but with males expressing more concern overall. Amongst blacks, however, there was no association between concern and duration. How can these findings be interpreted? Whilst the overall pattern seems to indicate that people pass through phases of differing concern, with the greatest concern being found in the medium term, this generalised pattern does not apply to all young people. In the early stages of unemployment the whites expressed more concern, especially so the white males, but after lengthy periods of unemployment they showed less concern, that is, resignation sets in equal to that of the blacks, which was at a constant level throughout.

Stigma from unemployment was assessed by asking them how much it troubled them that other people knew they were

Table 6.1: Duration of Unemployment and Concern About Their Own Unemployment

Question: How much does it trouble you that you're unemployed?
Responses: It doesn't trouble me at all (0), it troubles me a a bit (1), it troubles me a lot (2), it troubles me a great deal (3). Figures in this Table are average scores.

| | | Duration of Unemployment (Weeks) | | | | | | |
		<14 weeks	14-26	27-52	53-65	66-91	>91 weeks	Totals
Males:	Black	1.97	1.54	1.62	1.63	1.60	1.36	1.60
	White	1.65	1.79	1.87	1.47	1.54	1.65	1.67
Females:	Black	1.63	1.83	1.40	0.92	1.96	1.50	1.59
	White	1.85	1.56	1.67	1.52	1.20	1.21	1.49
Total sample		1.76	1.68	1.68	1.49	1.52	1.43	1.59

unemployed. The same statistical procedure was applied to this question as to the previous one, resulting in a slightly less significant relationship between stigma and duration (p <0.05). However, instead of a linear trend, as with concern, in this case there was an irregular 'up and down' pattern in the data, from which we conclude that there was no consistent progressive relationship between the variables.

2.2 Longitudinal Change in Psychological Well-being and Personality Between 1982 and 1983

GHQ change scores between 1982 and 1983 are shown in Table 6.2. The unemployed had a mean item score in 1983 which was only marginally significantly lower than the score they obtained in 1982. Considering the large sample size, we conclude that there was little change in their level of general psychological distress between the two interviews. In contrast to this, respondents who were employed in 1983 showed a significant decrease in their GHQ scores from the earlier level (from 1.03 to 0.58 for all those employed). Although employed respondents had significantly lower GHQ scores than those unemployed in 1983, they did not differ significantly from these respondents in 1982, when all were unemployed. This pattern of change gives us some confidence in asserting that the decrease in GHQ scores for those employed in 1983 was due to their gaining employment, and fails to support the alternative interpretation that they managed to gain employment because they were less distressed when they were unemployed.

Examination of the mean GHQ item scores of each of the four sub-groups shows a similar pattern of results, suggesting that employment is beneficial to the well-being of each of these groups. It can also be seen from Table 6.2 that unemployed white females had a significantly lower GHQ score in 1983 than they did in 1982. This was not found to be so for any of the other three sub-groups, and accounts for the overall marginally significant drop in GHQ scores. Longitudinal analysis of Depression and Anxiety measures revealed the same improvements in the employed and no change in the unemployed, with both groups being significantly different in 1983, but not different in 1982.

Further analyses showed that entering employment had a more marked impact on well-being (GHQ and Depression, not Anxiety) among females than among males, even though both sexes improved significantly.

Since the general hypothesis underlying this chapter is that more unemployment would lead to greater psychological distress, it was also decided to sub-divide those currently unemployed in 1983 into the continuously unemployed between 1982 and 1983 and those not continuously unemployed during that time period. Change in well-being was then compared

Table 6.2: Longitudinal Comparisons on Psychological Well-Being, Concern and Stigma Variables for Employed and Unemployed Respondents (U = unemployed, E = employed, p = significance level)

	Blacks Male			Blacks Female			Whites Male			Whites Female			Total		
	U	E	p	U	E	p	U	E	p	U	E	p	U	E	p
GHQ:															
t1	0.87	0.85	n.s.	1.01	1.10	n.s.	0.95	0.96	n.s.	1.07	1.17	n.s.	0.98	1.03	n.s.
t2	0.81	0.53	.001	1.10	0.65	.001	0.92	0.55	.001	0.98	0.61	.001	0.93	0.58	.001
p<	n.s.	.001		n.s.	0.01		n.s.	.001		0.05	.001		0.05	.001	
Depression:															
t1	1.04	1.05	n.s.	1.25	1.26	n.s.	1.14	1.13	n.s.	1.36	1.42	n.s.	1.20	1.24	n.s.
t2	1.04	0.62	.001	1.29	0.79	.001	1.17	0.55	.001	1.23	0.69	.001	1.18	0.64	.001
p<	n.s.	.001		n.s.	.001		n.s.	.001		0.05	.001		n.s.	.001	
Anxiety:															
t1	0.67	0.60	n.s.	0.89	0.95	n.s.	0.66	0.59	n.s.	0.97	0.98	n.s.	0.78	0.76	n.s.
t2	0.67	0.35	.001	0.97	0.62	.02	0.65	0.33	.001	0.90	0.55	.001	0.77	0.44	.001
p<	n.s.	0.01		n.s.	0.05		n.s.	.001		n.s.	.001		n.s.	.001	
Concern:															
t1	1.45			1.52			1.57			1.53			1.52		
t2	1.49			1.34			1.53			1.31			1.43		
p<	n.s.			n.s.			n.s.			0.01			n.s.		
Stigma:															
t1	0.77			0.63			0.66			0.77			0.72		
t2	0.67			0.46			0.43			0.50			0.51		
p<	n.s.			n.s.			0.01			.001			.001		

63

across the two groups. There were 353 who were continuously unemployed, and overall there were no significant changes in GHQ, Depression or Anxiety. The only suggestion of change within the sub-groups was a marginally significant (p = 0.05) reduction in Depression from a mean scale score of 8.19 to 7.47 amongst white females. Amongst the non-continuously unemployed there was a similar lack of change in affective well-being, with the single exception of black males, amongst whom GHQ scores fell from 0.99 to 0.77 (p <0.05).

It is possible that longitudinal changes in well-being were being masked by differences in the length of time respondents had been unemployed when first interviewed. Thus, if some people had been unemployed for a long period they may have already undergone a change in well-being as a result of their continuing unemployment. In their study of 954 unemployed men of all ages, Jackson and Warr (1984) found that the psychological health of men unemployed for more than three months was significantly worse than that found for those unemployed for shorter periods. Longitudinal analyses reported by Warr and Jackson (1985) showed that there is a significant increase in GHQ scores between interview points for men unemployed for less than three months at the first interview, but not for men unemployed for longer periods than this.

In order to test for such changes in this sample of young people, those continuously unemployed between interviews were divided into those who had been unemployed for up to three months at first interview, and those unemployed for longer than this at that time. Table 6.3 shows the mean well-being scores at both interviews for both groups. For the two groups as a whole, only one significant change was found: respondents unemployed for more than three months at time one showed a significant decrease in their GHQ scores over the following year. Similar analyses computed separately for the sex and ethnic sub-groups showed this decrease only occurred among white females. For the other groups the scores at both interview points were about the same. A similar decrease in Depression and Anxiety scores was found for white females unemployed for more than three months in 1982. In conclusion, these results do not support the findings reported by Warr and Jackson from their sample of men of all ages. Among young people of both sexes there is no sign of a decline in well-being at about three months of unemployment, while among young white females there is evidence that those unemployed for the longest periods actually show an increase in well-being.

For those employed in 1983 the questions on concern about and stigma from unemployment were not applicable, so results on this topic are restricted to those unemployed in 1983. Overall, there was no significant longitudinal change in concern about unemployment, but there was a significant fall (p <0.001) in the reported stigma from unemployment (see

Table 6.3: Longitudinal Analyses for Continuously Unemployed Between Interviews, Separated by Length of Unemployment at First Interview

| | | Blacks | | | Whites | | | | Total | |
| | | Male | Female | | Male | | Female | | | |
Length of Unemployment (Months)		<3	3+	<3	3+	<3	3+	<3	3+	<3	3+
GHQ:	t1	0.85	0.82	0.77	1.08	0.79	0.98	1.02	1.08	0.89	0.99
	t2	0.82	0.81	0.96	1.06	0.74	0.94	1.03	0.97	0.88	0.93
	p<								0.05		0.05
Depression:	t1	1.00	1.03	1.29	1.24	0.91	1.16	1.30	1.39	1.10	1.22
	t2	1.01	1.06	1.07	1.39	0.96	1.23	1.30	1.22	1.10	1.20
	p<								0.05		
Anxiety:	t1	0.66	0.69	0.76	0.86	0.48	0.71	0.95	1.07	0.71	0.84
	t2	0.70	0.62	1.09	0.90	0.53	0.71	1.07	0.92	0.81	0.78
	p<								0.05		
Sample size N		25	60	7	21	32	85	36	83	100	249

Table 6.2). In respect of sex and ethnic group differences, there was a moderately significant decrease in concern about unemployment amongst white females (p <0.01), who also reported less concern over unemployment at follow-up than did white males. The overall reduction in stigma was accounted for by both white males (significance p <0.01) and white females (significance p <0.001). Amongst the blacks there was no change. At follow-up the level of stigma amongst black males was moderately significantly higher than amongst white males (p <0.05).

This pattern of results falls into place with the cross-sectional analysis of the relationship between unemployment duration, concern and stigma. They showed how concern amongst whites was higher than among blacks in the early stages but after lengthy periods of unemployment fell to that of blacks. In the longitudinal analysis change has been shown amongst the whites, in terms of a fall in concern among females and a fall in stigma among all whites, but no change was seen among the blacks.

Turning to the measures of personality we found a number of differences between the unemployed and the employed. For those continuously unemployed between 1982 and 1983 there was no significant change in sociability or achievement orientation. Likewise for those unemployed also in 1983, but not continuously so between the interview points. However, for those in employment in 1983 there was a significant increase (p <0.001) in achievement orientation (see Table 6.4), a trend that was reflected in all sub-groups other than black females. No significant longitudinal changes were found in the sociability dimension.

Personality measures were also analysed by labour market histories, not just in 1983, but also in 1982 with the sample grouped by their labour market experience in 1983. In respect of sociability, the employed had significantly higher scores in 1983 than the continuously unemployed, whereas in 1982 there were no significant differences between the groups. And in respect of achievement orientation, in 1983 there was a significant contrast between the employed and the other two groups, whereas in 1982 there were no differences of statistical significance. These two sets of findings imply that employment led to higher achievement orientation, rather than the converse.

This result seems to be contrary to expectations, in that one would expect a previously higher level of achievement orientation to result in greater labour market success. It is worth considering, however, that these young people have little or no experience of working conditions, and in general they have been low achievers at school. Consequently their expectations and aspirations about the future are limited, and what we are seeing here is the development of a motivation to achieve as a result of early success in the labour market.

Table 6.4: Longitudinal Changes in Personality by Labour Market History

		Continuously Unemployed	Non-Continuously Unemployed	Employed at t2	Totals
Sociability:	t1	11.79	11.81	12.10	11.89
	t2	11.74	11.98	12.33	11.97
Achievement orientation:	t1	10.68	10.95	11.21	10.90
	t2	10.64	11.11	11.84	11.10

3. DISCUSSION OF THE RESEARCH FINDINGS ON WELL-BEING, PERSONALITY AND UNEMPLOYMENT

This chapter has examined the well-being of young people with varying lengths of continuous unemployment, up to two and a half years maximum. Despite exhaustive statistical analysis to test for linear and curvilinear relationships, no overall association (that is, among the whole sample) was found between unemployment duration and general psychological distress, depression or anxiety. The only statistical test to reach even moderate significance was on males, amongst whom the greatest distress was found in the shortest and in the longest unemployment duration categories (that is, a curvilinear relationship). However, this was only just statistically significant, at the $p < 0.05$ level. Considering the large sample size of this study, this one finding is considered to be of only minor importance. Thus, with a large sample, the results confirm earlier findings (e.g. Feather and Davenport, 1981; Warr, Jackson and Banks, 1982; Finlay-Jones and Eckhardt, 1984), that for the 16-18 year age group length of unemployment and psychological well-being are not directly related. Furthermore, neither was there any psychological deterioration amongst the unemployed, as assessed by longitudinal measures, between the first and second years in the labour market. This is all the more surprising since analyses controlled for whether or not individuals were continuously unemployed. The fact that longer spells of unemployment do not lead to progressive psychological decline applies equally to males and females, blacks and whites. It seems therefore that this finding would indicate that an adjustment to unemployment has been made, even though, as in previous studies (Banks et al., 1980; Banks and Jackson, 1982), when compared with the employed, the young unemployed report significantly more psychological distress.

We would also regard these results as yet further evidence that the phase model does not apply in its existing form to this age group. Even among older age groups its validity is still questioned (Warr, 1984a), and a more appropriate model would include a gradual decline in psychological health during the first months of unemployment, with some stabilisation at a lowered level at about six months (Jackson and Warr, 1984).

Another important question arising from this research is whether or not the experience of unemployment causes psychological impairment. There are a number of alternative ways of answering the question of causality. Earlier research has focussed on controlling for differences prior to entering the labour market, whilst the young people are still at school (e.g. Banks and Jackson, 1982; Patton and Noller, 1984). The clear conclusion from these studies is that the experience of unemployment is more likely to create increased psychological symptoms, rather than the converse. Another facet of the causality issue is whether the transition from unemployment to employment is accompanied by beneficial psychological changes. (This question of reversibility, however, is quite independent of an initial negative impact of unemployment. Unemployment could still be causally implicated even if, and arguably more important, no reversibility of effect occurred.) An earlier study of a smaller sample found this to be so (Jackson, Stafford, Banks and Warr, 1983), but called for replication on larger samples. The present study provides such, and clearly identifies the beneficial and reversible effects associated with moving into employment. The increased risk of "GHQ caseness" was a factor of 2.7 for the unemployed compared to employed. This applied equally to males and females. The percentage falling into this category was 29.9% male unemployed, 40.9% females unemployed, 11.2% male employed and 15% female employed. Furthermore, there was convincing evidence that psychological symptoms occurred after the start of unemployment and roughly half were specifically attributed to unemployment (see also, Warr, Banks and Ullah, 1985). It would seem therefore that there is now very strong evidence pointing to unemployment as a major factor in psychological impairment in this age group.

A further interesting question arises as to the extent to which this sample of young people differs from other unemployed samples in terms of their level of psychological well-being. Data from a number of other studies are available to enable comparisons of GHQ scores to be made with the same age group and also with older samples.

The most direct comparisons with a group of the same age and educational qualifications are provided by a two cohort study in the City of Leeds (Banks and Jackson, 1982), in which the GHQ-12 was administered as in the present study. Comparative data are shown in the following table:

	Mean GHQ-12 Scale Scores	
	Male	Female
Banks and Jackson, 1982:		
A3) Up to two and a half years after	13.9	14.6
B3) leaving school, currently unemployed	12.7	14.7
Present study: Unemployed in 1983	10.7	12.5

These data indicate the lower GHQ scores of the present sample, compared to the cohorts selected in 1978-79. This suggests that unemployment had a greater personal impact on school leavers earlier in the recession (in 1981) than later

69

on in the 1980s, when possibly there had been a collective adjustment to poor employment prospects.

For comparisons with older age groups the most appropriate sample is that of Payne, Warr and Hartley (1984). They report GHQ-12 data on 203 middle class and 196 working class men, drawn from those registered at 54 Unemployment Benefit Offices in mainland UK. All were white, married, registered unemployed for 6-11 months inclusive, and aged 25-39. The significant finding was the considerably higher GHQ scores than in the present sample, 15.37 for the middle class, and 15.06 for the working class; this suggests that for not dissimilar durations of unemployment the association with psychological distress was more marked in the 25-39 age group than in the 17-18 age group.

Two other studies (Jackson and Warr, 1984; White, 1983) offer potential comparison with the present study, but to effect this some reworking of the data was necessary. The Jackson and Warr study used the GHQ-30 on a sample 954 unemployed men, stratified by age and duration of unemployment. Age was found to be significantly related to GHQ scores such that the 20-59 age group had higher scores than the 16-19 and the 60-64 age groups. Extrapolation from the GHQ-30 (by dividing the total score by 30 and multiplying by 12) indicates that the 20-59 age group would have a GHQ-12 mean of 14.88, whilst the means for the 16-19 and 60-64 groups would be 12.25 and 10.44 respectively. This comparison again suggests that psychological impairment is less for the young and those reaching retirement age, and greatest for the 20-59 age group. In this latter group GHQ was also related to duration of unemployment. A further study which, with appropriate adjustments to the data, provides a comparison is of a national sample of long term unemployed (White, 1983), both males and females. Unfortunately, this latter study used the 0/1 scoring method on the GHQ, and results are not presented by age. The mean GHQ score (0/1 scoring) for males who were always out of work was 3.2, and 3.1 for those who had worked at some time. The equivalent values for females were 2.8 and 3.3. As expected from other studies, those in employment had significantly lower GHQ scores (White, 1983, tables 1X.13 and 1X.14). The equivalent values from the present study at time two are 2.1 for males, and 3.1 for females. The age structure of White's study was 17 to 64 for males, 17 to 59 for females, but unfortunately the GHQ results were not disaggregated by age. So although the GHQ values in the present study and in White's look quite similar it is impossible to say whether this applied to all age groups or indeed all durations of unemployment.

This section has focussed quite specifically on a selected subjective experience during unemployment. The variables essentially describe what the impact of unemployment is like. Such an analysis is thus of great importance.

However, it now needs to be harnessed to other concepts to explain how adjustment to unemployment does or does not take place. This linkage is made in Chapter 7, in which we investigate how and why some young people are better able to cope with unemployment than others. But before that we describe the basic results relating to labour market attitudes. This is contained in the following chapter.

Chapter 7

UNEMPLOYMENT, LABOUR MARKET ATTITUDES AND MOTIVATION TO SEEK WORK

We are told that unemployment means despair. But I'm loving every minute of it.

I've hardly worked since leaving school two years ago and manage comfortably on my £20.50 a-week dole money.

Work is boring and eats at your imagination and mind. Leisure is much more enjoyable and I spend my time reading, walking and meeting people, etc. Now that summer's on the way - and there are no jobs about - the unemployed should lay back and relish their freedom.
Letter to the Daily Mirror, 7 May, 1982

Teenagers new target for dole cuts

The government is considering plans to cut the dole paid to unemployed young people living with their parents.... The plans, part of the current Whitehall review of future public spending, seem certain to win the enthusiastic support of the Prime Minister. Mrs. Thatcher believes that some school leavers are tempted to stay on the dole rather than look for jobs. "They like it. They have a lot of money in their pockets," Mrs. Thatcher said earlier this summer.

The Sunday Times, 21 August, 1983

These two passages reflect public concern about young people's attitudes towards unemployment, and their motivation to seek employment when out of a job. Deacon (1978), in his review of the "scrounging controversy" of the 1970s, has argued that public concern that the unemployed did not want to work far outstripped concern over issues such as crime, industrial relations, taxation or world peace. But what is the truth behind these stereotypes? Is there any sound empirical evidence of young unemployed people preferring life on the dole? And what do the data from our own study tell us?

72

In fact there are a number of different issues contained in the "workshy" stereotype. These need to be distinguished before we can begin to answer questions such as these. A distinction needs to be made between not looking for a job because one prefers to remain unemployed, and not looking for a job because one believes it to be a fruitless exercise. The first of these alternatives concerns the notion of a work ethic, and its possible demise among young people. The second is concerned with discouragement. This may arise both as a response to earlier failure to find work and from low expectations of future attempts being successful. It is also possible to distinguish a third reaction to unemployment which results in little or no effort being made to find a job. This reaction is one of fatalism. The unemployed person has fatalistically accepted a life of being on the dole. He or she differs from the person experiencing discouragement, since the latter would still like to obtain a job. And unlike the person who actually enjoys being unemployed, the fatalist is someone who has simply learnt to tolerate it.

The extent to which such types of people actually exist, or are simply the product of the popular press or conventional wisdom, needs to be questioned. We will review the evidence from the sociological and psychological literature on these issues. At the same time we will show how far our own data support or refute these images. We will then go on to outline some of the psychological processes which we believe occur as reactions to unemployment and which may explain differences in the levels of job-seeking behaviour among the young people in our sample.

1.   ATTITUDES TO EMPLOYMENT AND UNEMPLOYMENT

The literature on work values and work salience is very extensive (see, for example, reviews by Kidd and Knasel, 1980, and by Cook, Hepworth, Wall and Warr, 1981). Most prominent in this literature are studies of the Protestant work ethic.

The concept of the Protestant work ethic has a long history, dating back to Weber's (1904) original formulation. The ethic itself is said to have been with us since the sixteenth century, when the religious significance of work served as the motivation for some of the middle classes and lay behind their subsequent rise to economic power and prosperity (Kelvin and Jarrett, 1985). In recent times it has been used as an explanatory variable by social scientists investigating a wide variety of issues (Furnham, 1982). In such studies the Protestant work ethic has usually been measured by multi-item scales (Blood, 1969; Mirels and Garrett, 1971). Scores on these scales have been correlated with personality measures, various attitude scales, and a wide range of work-related behaviours and concepts.

73

We are concerned here with the extent to which the absence of a work ethic can be detected among the young unemployed. It has been suggested by some (e.g. Jahoda, 1982) that there has been a general decline in the work ethic, particularly over the last fifty years. The return of high levels of unemployment has been seen as precipitating a shift from an emphasis on the importance of work and employment, and towards alternative ways of using one's time. Kelvin and Jarrett (1985) have argued that the existence of such an ethic is largely a myth anyway. They say that most people work purely for the means to support themselves, and that people would not work if they had some alternative source of income.

In fact this issue was put to people in a study reported by Warr (1982). Random samples of 2,149 men and 1,206 women were asked if they would work if they were to get, from some other source, enough money to live comfortably for the rest of their life. Contrary to Kelvin and Jarrett's (1985) claim, the majority of employed men and women in the sample said they would continue to work. Among unemployed men in the sample, 62% said they would work if it was not financially necessary. The corresponding figure among unemployed women was 40%. Among 16-24 year-olds, the majority (up to 80%) of men and women, employed and unemployed, said they would work without financial need. Findings from other studies of unemployed young people also fail to support the "workshy" stereotype. Feather and Davenport (1981) used a measure of "employment valence", which included items such as "Should a job mean more to a person than just money?". They found that mean scores on this scale were above the mid-point (indicating greater valence), even among those young people reporting no depressive affect due to being unemployed. Feather and Bond (1983) used the same measure on samples of employed and unemployed graduates, and also found mean scores to be above the mid-point of the scale. Moreover, no significant differences between the two groups were found, with unemployed respondents scoring as high as employed respondents. Jackson et al. (1983) used a six-item measure of "employment commitment" in their longitudinal study of Leeds school leavers. On a scale from one to five, mean item scores were above four on each of the five measurement occasions of this study. Tiggemann and Winefield (1980) measured the attitudes to work of intending school leavers in Australia, and re-interviewed these people after they had left school. They found that 87% said at the first interview that they would work if they inherited sufficient money to live comfortably. At the second interview, no significant difference was found in this respect between those who were in jobs and those who were unemployed. The authors conclude that "the work ethic is well accepted by young people, both as students and when they have left school. And it is shared by the young employed and the young unemployed alike" (Tiggemann and Winefield, p.275).

The results, therefore, "contradict the suggestion that there has been a decline in the work ethic among the young" (ibid, p.271). Roberts et al. (1981) report that even among those who do not register themselves as unemployed (typically assumed to be among the most alienated of the jobless) there is a strong desire for work. Similarly Millham, Bullock and Hosie (1978), on the basis of a number of studies of adolescents and covering many hundreds of interviews, conclude that "all of the adolescents we interviewed ... perceived work as very important" (p.13).

There is little support, then, for the view that the majority of unemployed young people do not want to be employed. This is further supported by the results from our own study. We used a modified version of the employment commitment scale described by Jackson et al. (1983) to measure a person's commitment to paid employment. We found that scores on this scale were well above the mid-point on both interview occasions and for both employed and unemployed people, suggesting high levels of commitment. For example, over three-quarters of the unemployed respondents interviewed at time two agreed with the statement "Even if I won a great deal of money, I would still want to have a job". Their scores on this scale were no lower than the scores of those who were employed at time two, and, among white females in our sample, the unemployed scored higher than the employed. When one considers that these young people had been unemployed for an average of two-thirds of the two years since they left school, these results provide little support for the "workshy" hypothesis.

The two quotations given at the beginning of this chapter point to more than simply the lack of a work ethic, however. They imply that young people enjoy life on the dole. But is there any evidence of this? In fact there have been remarkably few attempts to consider whether there are any positive aspects of unemployment for those experiencing it (see Fryer and Payne, 1984, for a notable exception). There are two studies which suggest that there may be a minority among the young unemployed who do enjoy their current status. In the study of young Australians reported by Feather and Davenport (1981), respondents were asked: "When you think about being unemployed, how does it make you feel?" Five possible responses were offered, ranging from "really glad" to "really depressed". Of the 212 people taking part in the study, 20 (approximately 14%) chose the first of these categories. Responses to the question were compared with those to other questions, and the significance of only the overall associations reported. On the whole, less depression as a result of unemployment was associated with less confidence about getting a job immediately after leaving school, lower employment valence, and a greater likelihood of blaming oneself for one's unemployment. It appears that those people experiencing the least depressive affect were the ones who did not leave school with high expectations and so were not likely to experience the most disappointment as a result of their failure to get a job. In addition, they were less likely to view themselves as being at the mercy of powerful external forces (social, political, and economic). Feather and Davenport suggest that these people may simply view their unemployment to be due to their own lack of effort.

In a British study, Hendry, Raymond and Stewart (1984) conducted semi-structured interviews with employed and unemployed school leavers, as well as 15-16 year-olds who were still at school. The authors report that ten of the 72 unemployed people interviewed said that they preferred unemployment to having a job. All ten were boys, and although they all admitted unemployment could be boring at times, five said they enjoyed the freedom it offered and five said their unemployment had given them a useful "breathing space" in which to formulate and consider career plans.

There is, then, some evidence to suggest that a minority of young people may welcome being out of a job. This in itself is not remarkable. Few experiences in life are either wholly positive or wholly negative. For young unqualified people, jobs are likely to be characterised by low wages, insecurity, and unpleasant working conditions. In contrast, unemployment at this age may not entail serious financial worries or be socially isolating. Given these factors, the important point to emphasise in both of these studies is that the vast majority of those interviewed did not view unemployment at all favourably. In the words of Hendry et al. (1984), the majority (86%) "saw unemployment as an unpleasant and unsatisfactory period of their lives. They described the experience as boring, soul-destroying and frustrating" (p.181).

Despite these two studies, there is still very little known about the positive aspects of unemployment. For example, no attempt has been made to measure positive attitudes to unemployment in the way that positive attitudes to employment have been measured in the studies of the work ethic. Also it is important to compare systematically on a range of variables those who do enjoy their unemployment with those who do not enjoy it. Do the former exhibit better psychological health than the latter? How do they spend their time? These are two of the aims that we set ourselves in our study of young unemployed people.

Positive attitudes to unemployment were measured by a five-item scale, producing a measure of "unemployment orientation". The alpha coefficient of internal reliability was 0.65, and the range of the scale was from five to twenty-five. High scores indicated a more positive orientation to unemployment. In fact the mean score obtained for all those who were unemployed at time two was low (10.33, s.d. = 4.11), providing little evidence that large proportions of our sample were enjoying their experience of unemployment. This can be seen more clearly when we consider responses to individual items in the scale. Each item consisted of a statement expressing a positive view of some aspect of unemployment. Respondents were required to indicate their level of agreement, using a response dimension ranging from 'strongly disagree' to 'strongly agree'. Most support, with a third of the sample expressing agreement, was found for the statement "There are plenty of interesting things for unemployed people to do." A quarter of those unemployed in 1983 agreed with the statement: "I like the freedom of being unemployed", and one-fifth agreed that "Unemployment is more pleasant than most people think it is." Only 6% agreed that "All things considered, being unemployed is usually better than having to go to work."

Using open-ended questions we also asked unemployed respondents to cite the advantages they feel they have over young people in jobs, and also any positive effects unemployment has had on them. The advantages to unemployment were generally seen to lie in the freedom that it brought. Over one-fifth of the respondents in 1983 cited greater personal control as the main advantage they possessed over those in jobs. A further 14% said they enjoyed not having to get up early in the morning, or that they enjoyed being able to stay up till late at night. No other responses attracted more than a handful of replies. However, over 40% of the sample said they could not think of any way in which unemployed people were better off than employed people.

A different pattern was found when respondents were asked if unemployment had had a positive effect on them. Almost 85% of the sample said it had not. Five percent of respondents said they felt they had grown more mature, or independent, as a result of their unemployment, and the same proportion said it had made them more determined, more eager to succeed.

It seems that although more than half of those unemployed in 1983 could perceive advantages to unemployment, few felt that it had had any positive effect on them. But who were those who perceived advantages to unemployment? Were they relatively happy on the dole, unwilling to look for a job? When we examined the gender and ethnicity of those responding to these items we found that black females were significantly more likely than white females to say there were advantages to unemployment, and white males were more likely than white females to cite positive effects due to unemployment. Of all the four sub-groups, it appeared that white females were the least likely to respond positively to these two items.

We then compared those who perceived advantages to unemployment with those who did not on a range of variables. Those perceiving advantages had significantly lower scores on the GHQ, Depression and Anxiety scales. They also had significantly lower levels of employment commitment and higher unemployment orientation scores. However, they did not differ on variables measuring their reported job seeking behaviour, such as the number of job applications they had made, the number of ways they were looking for work, and their own report of how hard they were looking for a job. Those respondents perceiving advantages to unemployment also reported being more able to fill their time, greater day-to-day variety in their lives, spending more time out of the house, and were more likely to report planning their days in advance. This type of constructive activity tends to be associated with lower levels of distress during unemployment (see Chapter 8).

In interpreting this pattern of results it is important to keep several points in mind. First, although those perceiving advantages to unemployment had better well-being than those seeing no advantages to unemployment, they still were significantly more distressed than employed people. For example, their mean item GHQ score was 0.91, compared with 1.03 for those not perceiving any advantages, and 0.58 for employed respondents. It is clear, then, that they still experienced elevated levels of psychological distress in comparison with those who had jobs. Another point relates to differences in labour market attitudes. Respondents perceiving advantages to unemployment could be expected to have a higher level of unemployment orientation, since the items on this scale are themselves concerned with the favourable aspects of unemployment. Although the employment commitment of those perceiving advantages was lower than that of those not doing so, there were no differences between the two groups on any of the variables measuring reports of job seeking behaviour. It is possible that the people who reported advantages to unemployment were those who were making the most out of their present situation. They appear to have been using their spare time constructively, planning their activities in advance and varying the things they did. As such they displayed fewer symptoms of psychological ill-health, even though they still differed significantly from young employed people. However, getting a job still appeared to be important to them, and they were putting as much effort into finding a job as were those who saw no advantages to unemployment.

Those who felt that their experience of unemployment had changed them for the better appeared to be quite different from those perceiving advantages to unemployment. They formed only a small minority (only 15% of the unemployed sample in 1983) and did not exhibit better psychological health than those who did not feel their unemployment had had any positive effect. They differed from the latter in their commitment to finding a job. Unlike those who perceived advantages to unemployment, those who felt they had benefited from the experience tended to be more committed to finding a job. They had made significantly more job applications than those not reporting any positive effects, and used more methods of looking for work. They also differed from those not reporting any positive effects from unemployment in terms of being able to plan their days in advance and reporting more day-to-day variety. If unemployment does have a positive effect on people, therefore, it appears that it makes them more determined to get a job. However, if the greater job seeking activity of those spurred on in this way does not prove to be successful it is possible they may become even more disaffected or depressed than those not having gone through this process.

In conclusion, there were some young people in our sample who appeared to be making the most of the free time brought about by their unemployment, and there were some who felt they had benefited in some way from being unemployed. However, it would not be correct to say that either found unemployment attractive. Both groups were still committed to escaping from the dole queue, and both displayed elevated levels of psychological ill-health. It would seem that there were very few indeed who did not prefer to have a job.

2. DISCOURAGED WORKERS IN THE LABOUR MARKET

We have seen that there is no real evidence of large numbers of young people enjoying life on the dole. Yet it would seem remarkable if, among those who still very much wanted to get a job, there were not some who had become so discouraged that they had simply given up looking for one. If we look only at the effort a person is putting into finding employment - the number of job applications they are making and so on - there is very little to distinguish the individual who does not want to work because he or she prefers unemployment from the person who has given up looking for a job because their chances of obtaining one are so slim. In both cases the level of job seeking is likely to be low. Yet it would be wrong to infer that an unemployed person who is not looking for work necessarily prefers to be unemployed. Hence it is important to look beyond outward appearances, and to consider cognitive variables such as attitudes, expectations, and perceptions, in order to determine whether discouragement is the reason for the behaviour.

The term "discouraged worker" originates from North America. Flaim (1973) has defined discouraged workers as "those persons who want work but are not looking for a job because of a belief that their search would be in vain" (p.8). In fact this makes use of quite a broad definition of discouragement. There may be many different reasons for believing one's changes of finding a job are slim. In population surveys conducted in the United States, a person may be classified as a discouraged worker if they believe there are no jobs in their own particular line of work, or if they feel they lack basic skills, or if they have some personal handicap which prevents them from securing most types of employment (Flaim, 1973). What we are concerned with here is a more specific phenomenon. It is the gradual discouragement which may come after repeatedly unsuccessful attempts to obtain a job. It is likely to be characterised by an increasingly negative attitude towards the utility of continued job seeking, and perhaps may be reflected in cynical attitudes towards other, more general aspects of the position of young people in the labour market. Before we discuss whether such processes are at work in our own sample, it is necessary to first consider the evidence from other studies of unemployed people.

The notion that unemployed people grow more discouraged as a result of their continued unemployment can be shown to be based upon a stage-account of the experience of unemployment. Such an account became popular during the 1930s, and is probably best summarised in Eisenberg and Lazarsfeld's (1938) review of psychological research into unemployment during that period:

> We find that all writers who have described the course of unemployment seem to agree on the following points: First there is shock, which is followed by an active hunt for a job, during which the individual is still optimistic and unresigned; he still maintains an unbroken attitude. Second, when all efforts fail, the individual becomes pessimistic, anxious, and suffers active distress; this is the most crucial state of all. And third, the individual becomes fatalistic and adapts himself to his new state but with a narrower scope. He now has a broken attitude.
> (Eisenberg and Lazarsfeld, 1938, p.378)

The unemployed individual, then, is typically seen as passing through stages of optimism and pessimism, and arriving at a position of fatalism (Beales and Lambert, 1934). Although there has been some disagreement concerning the number of stages and their precise nature (estimates range from two to seven - see Fryer and Payne, 1986), stage accounts can still be found in more recent studies of unemployment (e.g. Harrison, 1976; Hill, 1978).

Evaluation of the stage account of unemployment, both theoretical and empirical, has typically focussed on its implications for psychological well-being and not on its implications for job seeking. Fryer and Payne (1986), for example, point out that any improvement in well-being during the optimism phase may only be relative to the poor psychological health that can exist immediately prior to, and in anticipation of, job loss (Kasl et al., 1975). Similarly, Warr et al. (1982) suggest that "it seems plausible to assume that the decline in well-being following unemployment is gradual.... For example, unemployed workers may become more discouraged over time by continuing failures in job-seeking..." (p.207). This possibility is then tested empirically by examining the GHQ scores of individuals experiencing varying lengths of unemployment. Although one may accept Warr et al.'s claim that "observed differences in well-being at different lengths of unemployment are essential to any stage model" (p.212), it is also important to look for evidence of changes in the attitudes and behaviour of the unemployed individual. For example, the model implies that an unemployed person's attitude towards actually looking for a job may become increasingly negative. This in turn may be reflected in fewer attempts being made to find work. A person at the pessimistic stage may, however, still be expected to be committed to obtaining employment. That is, no decline may have taken place in his or her employment commitment as a result of continuing unemployment. In contrast, fatalism implies that the person has accepted their unemployment. This aspect is contained in the following account given by an unemployed man and quoted in Marsden and Duff (1975):

> I stopped even looking for a job. In them two years I lost all bloody interest. I thought, 'What's the bloody point of it all, anyway? What's the reason for it all?

The assumption of a stage model, and of growing discouragement, is often implicit in descriptions of the long-term effects of continuing unemployment. For example Kelvin and Jarrett (1985) state unequivocally that:

> Psychologically the most critical period for an unemployed individual is that between the initial stage of confidence that one will find work and a final state of tacit or even avowed resignation to unemployment.
>
> (Kelvin and Jarrett, 1985, p.27)

The authors assume that one of the key factors in encouraging this development is the disappointment which comes from repeated failures to secure a job, since "between confidence and resignation is the search for work and its failure" (ibid, p.27). The suggestion that resignation is the final destination of the unemployed individual is also contained in a report by the Manpower Services Commission (1981b). The report suggests that following an initial period of optimism, the unemployed person then enters a time of determined job seeking accompanied by continued rejection and a lowering of self-esteem. According to the report, if unemployment continues, the individual finally becomes resigned to the state of joblessness: "although job seeking continues, it is at a reduced level and with little real optimism of finding a job.... there is a general feeling of resignation and of inferiority" (MSC, 1981b, p.9).

There are a number of empirical studies in which some attempt has been made to investigate whether unemployed people grow more discouraged as a result of their failure to find a job. These typically involve looking for an association between the length of time a person has been unemployed and the value they place on being employed. Feather (1982), for example, found that his measure of Protestant ethic values was not significantly correlated with the length of unemployment experienced among his sample of young Australians. However, a measure of the level of job seeking ("How frequently do you look for a job?") was negatively correlated with unemployment duration. Hence those respondents who had been unemployed for the longest length of time still valued employment as highly as those recently made unemployed, although they tended to be looking less hard for a job. Feather and Barber (1983) found that their single-item measure of employment valence was not significantly correlated with unemployment duration in their sample of unemployed people (mean age 20.06 years), and remained high for most respondents. Although the present confidence the respondents reported about finding a job was lower than initial confidence prior to leaving school (recalled retrospectively), it was not correlated with the length of time they had been unemployed. Hence there was no evidence that those who had been unemployed for the longest periods tended to value employment less than those recently unemployed, or that they had lower expectations of success.

Evidence apparently consistent with the "discouraged worker" hypothesis has been reported in another Australian study. Feather and Davenport (1981) report finding "observed decreases in levels of expectation, effort, and motivation from leaving school to the present time, decreases that can be related to the failure to get stable employment despite attempts to do so over a considerable period" (p.430). They interpret their results as being consistent with an "expectancy-valence" analysis of unemployment, which predicts that "repeated failure to get a job will determine reduced expectations of success and decreases in the tendency to seek employment" (p.430). However, the results from this study must be interpreted with some caution. Respondents were asked to recall their initial expectations and efforts to find a job when they left school. These retrospective reports were then compared with their current reports, resulting in the reductions reported by the authors. Clearly the results would be more persuasive if longitudinal data had been used to show a real decline in these variables. In addition to this, Feather and Davenport failed to find any significant association between length of time unemployed and their measures of expectation, employment valence and motivation to work. Once again then, there is no evidence of lower expectations, values or effort among those people experiencing the longest periods of unemployment.

Two British studies shed further light on this issue. In their study of Leeds school leavers, Warr et al. (1982) report that employment commitment was negatively correlated with duration of unemployment. However, the association was present mainly among females, and the authors suggest that this was due to their withdrawal from the labour market because of pregnancy or childcare. There is no evidence, therefore, of increased discouragement due to prolonged unemployment. In Warr's (1982) earlier study, in which random samples of men and women were asked if they would continue to work if it were no longer financially necessary, there is some evidence of discouragement among the young unemployed. Sixty-one per cent of those reporting that they were not looking for a job said they would work without financial incentives. Warr concludes that it is "likely that some members of the sub-group judge that in a setting of extremely high local unemployment there is at present no point in seeking a job; however their commitment to paid employment remains high" (p.301). We see here, then, signs that young people may have given up looking for work. This does not appear to be because they enjoy their unemployment, or because they have given up any desire to have a job, but because they have become discouraged from looking for work due to the low probability of success.

This distinction between those people who no longer value employment and those who do but are discouraged from looking for it, is an important one. The studies reviewed here typically show that there is no significant association between the value placed on employment and the length of time spent unemployed. In other words, there is no evidence of a decline in these values, yet clearly there may still have been an increase in discouragement. In order to determine whether this is the case we need to look at other variables, such as attitudes towards looking for work, expectations of obtaining a job, the current level of job-seeking, and so on. Few studies have attempted to measure these or to see if they are related to the length of time spent unemployed. In our own study, the issue of "discouraged workers" was investigated in three ways.

Firstly, we carried out cross-sectional analyses of the association between the length of time a respondent had been unemployed and a number of other variables. These variables included measures of expectations of obtaining a job, attitudes towards specific aspects of the labour market, and reports of job-seeking behaviour, in addition to employment commitment. In this way we could look for signs of discouragement even if there was no evidence of a decline in the value placed on employment. We also included our measure of unemployment orientation, in order to see if there were signs that unemployment became more attractive the longer it was endured. The fact that some of the respondents had been continuously unemployed for two years also meant that we could look for evidence of discouragement among those experiencing particularly long periods of unemployment. Few studies have managed to obtain large numbers of people unemployed for this length of time. Failure to find evidence of discouragement may therefore have been partly due to insufficient time spans being considered. We were also intrigued by the possibility that even the value placed on employment (employment commitment) would begin to decline after such prolonged unemployment.

Secondly, we conducted longitudinal analyses on these variables. Most of the studies described above used cross-sectional designs, and therefore could not investigate the possibility of <u>changes</u> in the values of the variables they measured. For example, a negative correlation between length of unemployment and employment commitment would simply indicate that lower levels of employment commitment had been found among those who had been unemployed for the longest periods. It would not indicate that an actual decline in commitment had taken place, since it is possible that these people had low commitment upon becoming unemployed, and that this had contributed to their failure to secure a job in the time that followed. By focussing on those respondents who had been continuously unemployed between both interviews, and comparing their scores on certain variables measured in 1982 with scores obtained in 1983, we were able to see if there had been an actual change in these variables with prolonged unemployment.

A third aim was to examine for possible sex or ethnic differences in discouragement among the unemployed. There is considerable evidence that black people face discrimination when applying for jobs (e.g. Commission for Racial Equality, 1978; Dex, 1983; Smith, 1976; 1981). If discouragement arises out of successive failures to obtain a job, then we might expect black people in our sample to be more discouraged, or perhaps to become discouraged sooner, than white respondents. Women may also face discrimination in the labour market, and so may be more prone to discouragement than young men. However, it is also possible that some women withdraw from the labour market, adopting domestic or childcaring roles. There may be a variety of reasons for this, such as pressures from others in the family, frustration through unsuccessful attempts to find employment, or unplanned births or deaths. It was important, therefore, to look for differences between males and females in terms of the changes that occurred in the variables we measured.

2.1 Cross-sectional Analyses

The cross-sectional analyses involved drawing comparisons between respondents who had been unemployed for varying lengths of time. The analyses were computed for all those who were unemployed in 1983 (time two), and so included those who had been unemployed for the two years since they had left school. We used one-way analyses of variance to see if there was a statistically significant association between the variable being measured and the length of the current unemployment spell. This latter variable was divided into six categories, each covering at least 13 weeks of continuous unemployment. Where significant associations were found, further analyses were carried out to determine the categories between which the significant differences lay. Table 7.1 shows the mean scores of respondents in the six categories on a range of variables. These variables will now be discussed in turn.

The first four variables shown in Table 7.1 are concerned with the reported level of job-seeking. Each of these were found to be significantly related to the length of time unemployed when interviewed in 1983, with longer spells of unemployment being associated with lower levels of job-seeking. The first measure is the number of job applications the respondent reported making in the year prior to the interview. Approximately 44% of the sample in 1983 had made six or more job applications, with a further 29% reporting making between two and five applications. The percentage of respondents not having made any applications was 19. Table 7.1 shows the mean number of applications made by respondents in each of the six categories of unemployment duration. A highly significant association was found, and post hoc analyses showed that the significant differences lay between those categories where respondents had been unemployed for less than one year (i.e. the first three categories) and those unemployed for more than one year.

The second variable shown in Table 7.1 is the number of job applications respondents reported making in the four weeks prior to the interview. In 1983, 58% had made no applications in the previous four weeks, 16% had made one application, 10% had made two, and 15% had made three or more job applications. This variable was also significantly related to the length of time spent unemployed. Those who had been unemployed for up to 13 weeks reported making the most applications, and differed significantly in this respect from those in the two groups unemployed for more than 66 weeks.

Of course, the number of job applications a person makes in a specified period of time is partly dependent on the number of suitable jobs which become available in that period. A person may be looking hard for a job, without actually making any formal job applications. The next variable shown in Table 7.1 is thus measuring a different aspect of job-

85

Table 7.1: Mean Scores of Selected Variables for Increasing Durations of Unemployment

	No. of Weeks Unemployed						Significance Level
	<13	14-26	27-52	53-65	66-91	>91	p<
Job applications in last year	3.62	3.55	3.73	3.43	2.83	3.04	0.001
Recent job applications	1.36	1.08	1.25	0.89	0.74	0.82	0.001
No. of job search methods	3.70	3.45	3.52	3.17	2.70	2.79	0.001
Current job seeking	2.56	2.42	2.40	2.25	2.21	2.19	0.001
Job expectations	3.41	3.15	2.95	2.84	2.62	2.60	0.001
Employment commitment	25.87	25.57	25.66	24.80	25.87	26.11	n.s.
Unemployment orientation	9.79	10.04	10.22	11.14	10.33	10.62	n.s.
Disaffection with youth labour market	18.15	19.55	19.14	19.95	20.26	20.86	0.001
Job search attitude	12.30	11.43	11.45	11.08	10.28	10.22	0.001
N	177	152	181	137	181	180	

Note: N's are maximum and vary slightly according to the variable being measured.

seeking: the number of ways in which a person is looking for
a job.

We asked unemployed respondents to indicate the different
ways in which they had been looking for work during the four
weeks prior to the interview. We then simply counted the
number of different ways each of them had indicated. The mean
number of job search methods used is shown in Table 7.1. This
was significantly associated with the length of time spent
unemployed, and once again the significant differences lay
between those in the three categories of less than or up to
one year of continuous unemployment, and those in the three
categories of more than one year.

The number of job search methods used obscures other
potential differences in the intensity of job-seeking. During
the four weeks specified, one respondent may have made one
visit to the job centre and one visit to the careers office.
That person would thus have used more methods than a person
who had visited the job centre on every day of that month but
who had not used any other method of looking for work. Yet we
would normally want to say that the second person had a
higher level of current job-seeking. It is useful, therefore,
simply to compare respondents in terms of how they themselves
describe their current level of job-seeking. The fourth
variable shown in Table 7.1, current job-seeking, is based on
such a measure. All unemployed respondents were asked to
indicate which of the following statements best described
their position at that time: "I'm actively looking for a
job"; "I'm keeping my eyes open but not looking hard", and
"I'm not really looking at the present". Approximately half
of the unemployed sample in 1983 reported that they were
actively looking for a job, and only 25% said that they were
not really looking. The remainder, about one-third, said they
were keeping their eyes open but not looking hard. These
responses were then scored on a scale from one to three, with
a high score indicating a higher level of current job-seeking.
Table 7.1 shows that the mean scores on this variable were
also significantly associated with the duration of
unemployment. We can see that there are successively lower
levels of reported job-seeking with increasing durations of
unemployment.

There is no single index of job-seeking which can
accurately summarise how much effort a person is putting into
looking for a job. By using four separate measures we have
been able to examine different aspects of job-seeking, thus
overcoming the limitations of each when considered on its own.
Since all four were found to be significantly associated with
length of unemployment, we can be reasonably confident in
concluding that among those unemployed for the longest periods
we find much less effort being put into finding a job. This
is certainly consistent with the "discouraged worker"

hypothesis, though we cannot infer from these analyses alone that there has been an actual <u>decline</u> in the level of job-seeking. Those long-term unemployed respondents may never have put much effort into job-seeking, and this would thus have been a major contributory factor in their continuing unemployment. Since the analyses are cross-sectional, we cannot tell whether long spells of unemployment are leading to reduced levels of job-seeking, or whether low levels of job-seeking are leading to longer spells of unemployment. In reality, both of these possibilities are likely to be partly true. We show later in this chapter, for example, that those respondents making the fewest job applications and using the least number of job search methods in 1982 are more likely to have failed to find a job by the time of the second interview in 1983. However, in the section which follows we describe the results from our longitudinal analyses which examined whether there had been an actual decline in the level of job-seeking of unemployed respondents from 1982 to 1983.

The remaining part of Table 7.1 shows the associations between length of unemployment and several attitudinal variables. The first of these is concerned with the respondents' expectations of finding a job in the near future. We asked unemployed respondents: "Do you expect to get a job within the next six months?" There were five response categories ranging from "Definitely not" to "Yes, definitely" and these were scored from one to five, such that a high score indicated higher expectations. Although only seven percent of those unemployed in 1983 thought they would definitely get job within the next six months, a further 34% thought it was "quite likely". Thirty percent thought they would "probably not" get a job, and 14% thought they definitely would not. About 15% were undecided. Table 7.1 shows there is a clear and significant association between this variable and duration of unemployment. Lower expectations of getting a job were found with successively longer spells of unemployment. Once again, we cannot infer from these analyses that a decline in expectations has taken place, though the results are consistent with the assumption that pessimism and resignation can be found amongst those unemployed for the longest periods.

Four multi-item scales were used to measure specific labour market attitudes in our sample. Table 7.1 shows the associations between these variables and length of unemployment. Both employment commitment and unemployment orientation were found to be unrelated to the length of time a person had been unemployed. The former can be seen to be high among respondents in each of the six categories of duration. Scores on this scale could range from a minimum of seven to a maximum of 35, and Table 7.1 shows that the mean for each category was above 24. Even among those experiencing two years of continuous unemployment there was still a strong desire to obtain a job. Hence we found no evidence that continuing unemployment led to a rejection of employment among the majority of our respondents.

A similar pattern was found with regard to unemployment orientation scores. These were found to be low (on a scale ranging from five to 25) for each category of duration. It seems that in addition to continuing to want a job, the long-term unemployed in our sample showed few signs of growing to like unemployment. Taken together, these two results provide strong evidence to refute the "workshy" hypothesis.

The analyses for the remaining two variables shown in Table 7.1 suggest that there may still be a growing sense of discouragement with continuing unemployment. The first of these variables, disaffection with the youth labour market, measures the extent of negative and cynical attitudes towards the youth labour market and the official agencies operating in it. Respondents were asked to indicate whether they agreed or disagreed with statements such as "People like me have no chance of finding a decent job", and "Most of the government's training schemes for unemployed young people are just a waste of time". On the whole, respondents tended to be divided in their opinions, with similar proportions agreeing and disagreeing with the items. There was one exception to this, with three-quarters of those unemployed in 1983 agreeing with the statement "Most employers look upon people like me simply as a form of cheap labour". Partly as a result of this, the overall mean score on the scale, 19.65 (s.d. 5.09), was above the mid-point of 18 (minimum six, maximum 30). The final variable, job search attitude, was more specific. This measured attitudes towards looking for work, and contained items such as "I'm looking for a job as hard as I've ever done" and "I can't be bothered looking for a job any more". Scoring on the latter type of item was reversed, so that a high score on this scale indicated a positive attitude towards looking for work. Low scores would be obtained if respondents tended to agree with statements like the latter. Hence low scores would indicate a generally discouraged attitude towards the utility of looking for work. The mean score of 11.11 (s.d. 3.31) obtained for all unemployed respondents was above the mid-point of 9 on the scale (minimum 3, maximum 15).

Table 7.1 shows that disaffection with the youth labour market and job search attitude were both significantly associated with duration of unemployment. There was a general upward trend in disaffection scores with increasing durations of unemployment. Comparisons between the various categories of duration showed that those three groups experiencing more than one year of continuous unemployment all had significantly higher levels of disaffection than those experiencing up to 13 weeks of unemployment.

In contrast, lower scores on the job search attitude scale were found with increasing durations of unemployment. Significant differences in this variable were found within a

89

relatively narrow band of unemployment duration, with respondents unemployed for between 27 and 52 weeks scoring significantly lower than those unemployed for up to 13 weeks. The two groups of respondents unemployed for more than 66 weeks both obtained scores which were significantly lower than those three groups unemployed for less than one year. Hence there are signs of increasingly negative attitudes towards looking for work with longer durations of unemployment.

Taken as a whole, the results shown in Table 7.1 are consistent with the notion of discouraged workers. They show that those people unemployed for long periods of time, when compared with those experiencing less unemployment, were putting significantly less effort into looking for work. However, this does not appear to be because they no longer wanted to have a job, since their level of employment commitment was high and was similar to that of those who had been unemployed for a much shorter length of time. Neither can it be said that the long-term unemployed had grown accustomed to their status and had begun to enjoy being without a job. Their unemployment orientation scores were low, and did not differ significantly from the scores of those experiencing less unemployment. However, disaffection with the youth labour market in general, and with the value of continued job hunting in particular, was significantly greater among those experiencing the longer spells of unemployment. These people were also significantly more pessimistic about their chances of finding a job in the near future. The figures shown in Table 7.1 show a clear trend in each of these variables, with reduced levels of job-seeking, expectations and positive job search attitude, and increased levels of disaffection, accompanying successively longer periods of unemployment. There is, therefore, evidence from these analyses to support the idea that young people who are unemployed for long periods of time are likely to become increasingly discouraged from seeking work.

2.2 Longitudinal Analysis
A more stringent test of the "discouraged worker" hypothesis is provided by analysing changes in the variables shown in Table 7.1. Cross-sectional analyses show that those unemployed for long periods appear to be more discouraged than those experiencing less unemployment, but they do not show that this discouragement results from increasing spells of unemployment. As suggested above, an alternative, and equally plausible interpretation is that their lengthier unemployment is itself the outcome of their lower levels of job-seeking. However, if it can be shown that those experiencing long spells of unemployment have not always been so discouraged, and that there has been an actual decline in their efforts to find a job, then this alternative explanation would become

less plausible. For this reason we carried out longitudinal analyses to see if there had been a change from 1982 to 1983 in respondents' scores on the variables being considered here. These analyses were compiled only for those people who had been continuously unemployed during that time (n = 353), so that any observed change could not be attributed to them having perhaps obtained a job or a place on YOP during that period.

Table 7.2 shows the mean scores in 1982 and 1983 on selected variables for those respondents who had been continuously unemployed between these two dates. On all four indices of job-seeking (the first four variables of Table 7.2) there had been a statistically significant decline from 1982 to 1983. That is, there had been a significant decrease in the amount of effort these people were putting into finding a job over the course of this year of continuing unemployment. If, in 1982, these people were making fewer attempts to find a job than those who subsequently obtained one (and this is suggested by the figures shown in Table 7.6), then this is likely to have been a factor contributing to their continuing unemployment. However, the fact that there has still been a decline in their level of job-seeking strongly suggests that there has been some effect in the opposite direction. That is, their continuing unemployment is likely to have contributed to a fall in the amount of effort they were putting into finding a job in 1983 when compared with that of 1982.

Table 7.2: Mean Scores in 1982 and 1983 of Continuously Unemployed Respondents

	1982	1983	p<
Job applications in last year	3.41	2.95	0.001
Recent job applications	1.06	0.71	0.001
No. of job search methods	3.14	2.72	0.001
Current job seeking	2.28	2.15	0.01
Job expectations	2.95	2.70	0.001
Employment commitment	25.78	25.49	n.s.
Unemployment orientation	10.30	10.40	n.s.
Disaffection with youth labour market	20.09	20.27	n.s.
Job search attitude	10.84	10.18	0.001

The question remains, does this drop in effort reflect a growing sense of discouragement or is it more likely to represent an adaptation to a state of joblessness? The remaining figures in Table 7.2 suggest that the first of these two possibilities is the most likely. These figures show that there had been a significant decline from 1982 to 1983 in the respondents' expectations of obtaining a job in the following six months, and it is possible that this reflects an increase in pessimism during that period. In contrast, there had been no significant change in scores on the attitude scales measuring employment commitment and unemployment orientation. Hence there is no evidence in these data that unemployed respondents were becoming less committed to the idea of having a job or that they were beginning to enjoy more their state of joblessness. This is consistent with the cross-sectional analyses shown in Table 7.1, which show employment commitment to be high and unemployment orientation to be low even among those experiencing the longest spells of unemployment.

Interestingly, Table 7.2 shows there was no significant change from 1982 to 1983 in the level of disaffection with the youth labour market, even though cross-sectional analyses had shown this to be associated with length of unemployment. Cross-sectional analyses carried out on the data obtained in 1982, and therefore comparing respondents with varying lengths of unemployment during the period from 1981 to 1982, suggest an explanation for this (see Ullah, 1985 for further details). These analyses show that differences in disaffection could be found between those respondents unemployed for only a short length of time (up to three months) when first interviewed and those unemployed for a moderate length of time (up to one year), with the latter having the highest disaffection scores. However, comparisons between those experiencing between nine and twelve months of unemployment and those unemployed for more than one year showed there were no significant differences in their level of disaffection. It is suggested by Ullah (1985) that disaffection among young people may 'level off' if their unemployment continues for a prolonged period of time. Since few respondents at that time (1982) had been unemployed for more than one year, and none had been so for more than about fifteen months, it was not possible to adequately test this possibility. However, the data shown in Table 7.1, containing people unemployed for between one and two years, support this suggestion. No significant differences in disaffection were found between any of the three categories of respondents experiencing more than one year of continuous unemployment, although all three had significantly higher levels of disaffection than those unemployed for up to three months. The lack of change in disaffection shown by the figures in Table 7.2 may thus be reflecting this stability for those people experiencing long spells of unemployment.

Finally, Table 7.2 shows that there had been a significant decline in the level of job search attitude between 1982 and 1983. Attitudes towards looking for jobs were therefore less positive in 1983 than they had been at the time of the first interview. Once again, this is consistent with the hypothesis that continuing unemployment leads to an increasingly negative view of the expedience of continued job hunting.

The cross-sectional analyses summarised in Table 7.1 suggested that respondents who had been unemployed for the longest periods were becoming increasingly discouraged from seeking work. However, there was an alternative explanation for these findings: namely that these respondents had been discouraged for some time and that this had caused, rather than resulted from, their continuing unemployment. The longitudinal analyses summarised in Table 7.2 have failed to support this alternative interpretation. The analyses confirmed that there had been significant changes in the level of job-seeking behaviour, expectations of obtaining a job, and attitudes towards looking for work for those respondents continually unemployed between the two interviews. The analyses also support the suggestion that such changes reflect an increasing sense of discouragement among these people. Although there was a fall in the amount of effort they were putting into finding a job, this did not appear to reflect a change in the value they placed on having a job or a more favourable attitude towards being unemployed. It is important to remember that no significant changes were found in either the level of employment commitment shown by respondents in 1982 and 1983, or in their attitudes towards being unemployed, as measured by the unemployment orientation scale. However, the expectations unemployed respondents had of obtaining a job in the coming six months, and their attitudes towards looking for work, became significantly less favourable during the course of their unemployment. Hence it is reasonable to suggest that the reason they were trying less hard to find a job in 1983 than in 1982 was that they had become increasingly discouraged from doing so. There is little evidence to suggest that they no longer wanted to have a job.

On the basis of cross-sectional analyses carried out on the 1982 data (Ullah and Banks, 1985) we have proposed a model of the psychological processes which may be involved when a person becomes increasingly discouraged from looking for work. It is suggested that long spells of unemployment lead to reduced levels of job-seeking through changes in expectations of obtaining a job and attitudes towards looking for one. As their unemployment continues, young people appear to become increasingly negative about their chances of obtaining a job in the near future and in their attitudes towards looking for work. Associated with such changes, are lower levels of job-seeking. In this light the behaviour of these young people

93

has a ring of rationality to it. A negative attitude towards looking for work and little expectation of obtaining it are understandable reactions to long spells of unemployment. They may also be sound reasons for scaling down one's level of job-seeking, since fruitless job hunting is likely to result in failure, frustration and loss of confidence (Feather and Barber, 1983).

2.3 Sex and Ethnic Differences

Comparisons between males and females, and between whites and blacks, were made on both the 1982 and the 1983 data. Since the 1983 sample contained an additional boost sample of 550 unemployed people, both data sets consisted of over one thousand unemployed young people. With such large samples it was possible to reliably compare sub-groups within those samples.

There were a number of statistically significant differences between white respondents and black respondents in 1982. In each case white respondents appeared to be more positive in their approach to finding a job. Thus, white males reported making significantly more job applications in the four weeks prior to being interviewed than did black males. Whites (both males and females) also reported using a greater number of ways of looking for work than did their black counterparts, and their own reports of their current level of job-seeking were higher than those reported by blacks. White respondents also had significantly higher expectations of obtaining a job in the next six months than did black respondents, this being true among males and among females. With regard to employment commitment, white males had a higher score than black males (indicating greater commitment), and a similar difference was found on the job search attitude scale (indicating a more positive attitude among white males). Black males, however, were found to have a significantly higher unemployment orientation score than white males, suggesting that they viewed their unemployment more favourably than did whites. No significant differences between whites and blacks, either among males or among females, were found on the scale measuring disaffection with the youth labour market. These results strongly suggest that in 1982, approximately one year after leaving school, unemployed whites in our sample were making greater efforts to find a job than were unemployed blacks, and that they were more positive in their attitudes towards obtaining work. This may have indicated greater discouragement among blacks, and this possibility will be discussed more fully below.

Only two statistically significant sex differences in these variables were found in 1982. Among black respondents only, females had a higher level of employment commitment than did males. Among both blacks and whites, males were found to have higher unemployment orientation scores than females. Both of these differences are contrary to the suggestion that females may withdraw from the labour market and adopt other roles. The fact that no significant differences were found on any of the job-seeking variables also fails to support this possibility.

A somewhat different pattern of results was found when the data obtained in 1983 were examined. Many of the ethnic differences found in 1982 were not present among the 1983 sample, with there being no significant differences between blacks and whites in terms of the numbers of recent job applications made, current job-seeking, job expectations, employment commitment, or job search attitude. White respondents in 1983 still reported using significantly more methods of looking for work than did blacks, although this was true only among males. Similarly, black males had significantly higher unemployment orientation scores than white males, as they had in 1982. There were also two ethnic differences in 1983 which had not been present in 1982: white males reported making significantly more job applications in the previous twelve months than did black males, and white females were more disaffected with the youth labour market than were black females. Yet taken as a whole, these results suggest that in a number of respects unemployed whites were no longer making a greater effort to find a job than were unemployed blacks, and that whites did not hold more positive attitudes towards employment (as measured by the employment commitment scale) or job-seeking than those attitudes held by blacks, as they had done in 1982.

There was also some evidence in 1983 that females were looking for a job less hard than were males, although there had been no evidence of this in 1982. Among whites, males reported a higher level of current job-seeking than did females, while among blacks and whites there were higher expectations of obtaining a job among males than among females. None of these differences between the sexes had been found in 1982. In addition to this there were no significant differences between males and females in terms of employment commitment or unemployment orientation, even though differences had been found in 1982, with females being more committed to employment and holding less favourable attitudes towards being unemployed. There was one further difference between males and females in 1983, with black males having higher disaffection scores than black females.

The results obtained from comparisons between blacks and whites, and males and females, which were made on the 1983 data were therefore somewhat different from those results obtained from the 1982 data. The nature of this difference suggests two patterns of change may have occurred during the period from 1982 to 1983. First, there is evidence of white respondents being more committed to finding a job than black respondents in 1982, but less evidence of this in 1983. Examination of responses to specific items showed that the proportion of white respondents making no job applications was higher in 1983 than in 1982, while the proportion reporting that they were actively looking for a job was smaller in 1983 than that found in 1982. The mean number of job search methods reported by whites was also smaller in 1983 than that found in 1982. These comparisons suggest that whites were less committed to job-seeking in 1983 than they were in 1982, and that this had resulted in there being fewer differences between blacks and whites in 1983.

A second pattern indicated by these analyses is that evidence of females withdrawing from the labour market is stronger in the 1983 data than it is in the 1982 data. For example, the proportions of females making no job applications in the twelve months prior to the interview had increased from 17.8% in 1982 to 27.1% in 1983 among blacks, and from 5.9% in 1982 to 19.1% in 1983 among whites. However, there were still many similarities in 1983 in the job-seeking and attitudes of males and females, and so there was no sign of large numbers of young women withdrawing from the labour market.

In order to see if these two patterns represented actual changes in the job-seeking strategies of whites and of females, we carried out additional longitudinal analysis. Once again these analyses were compiled only for those respondents who had been continuously unemployed between 1982 and 1983. The results of these analyses are shown in Table 7.3.

Comparisons between the figures for blacks and for whites support the interpretation of the cross-sectional analyses. It is white respondents who show a decline in their level of job-seeking from 1982 to 1983, with there being little or no change among blacks. Thus there was a significant decrease on all four measures of job-seeking among white respondents, both for males and for females. White respondents' expectations of obtaining a job in the next six months were also significantly lower in 1983 than they were in 1982. Although no significant changes were found in scores on the attitude scales measuring employment commitment, unemployment orientation and disaffection with the youth market (confirming the pattern shown earlier in Table 7.2), there was a significant change in job search attitude. Whites' attitudes towards looking for a job were significantly less positive in 1983 than they were in 1982.

No significant changes were found on any of these variables among black respondents. The relatively small number of continuously unemployed black females may account for why some of the larger differences between scores in 1982 and 1983 failed to reach statistical significance. Yet despite this there appears to be a considerable amount of stability in the scores of black respondents. Comparisons

Table 7.3: Mean Scores in 1982 and 1983 of Continuously Unemployed Respondents, by Sex and Ethnic Group

		Blacks		Whites	
		Males	Females	Males	Females
		(n=87)	(n=28)	(n=119)	(n=119)
Job applications	1982	3.18	3.14	3.56	3.50
in last year	1983	3.06	2.54	3.16	2.75
	p<			0.01	0.001
Recent job	1982	0.93	0.67	1.13	1.17
applications	1983	0.78	0.74	0.77	0.59
	p<			0.01	0.01
No. of job search	1982	2.92	2.57	3.36	3.23
methods	1983	2.92	2.43	2.88	2.49
	p<			0.01	0.001
Current job	1982	2.56	1.89	2.39	2.29
seeking	1983	2.34	2.14	2.24	1.92
	p<			0.05	0.001
Job expectations	1982	2.80	2.79	3.15	2.90
	1983	2.97	2.64	2.83	2.39
	p<			0.01	0.001
Employment	1982	25.02	27.81	25.50	26.17
commitment	1983	25.28	25.44	25.46	25.59
	p<				
Unemployment	1982	11.28	9.75	10.34	9.68
orientation	1983	11.27	10.04	10.28	10.10
	p<				
Disaffection with	1982	19.69	20.35	20.21	20.22
the youth labour	1983	19.70	19.00	20.88	20.24
market	p<				
Job search	1982	10.53	9.39	11.30	10.97
attitude	1983	10.40	10.04	10.65	9.61
	p<			0.05	0.001

between the figures obtained at both interviews for both blacks and whites supports the pattern of change suggested earlier. Mean scores of black respondents are generally lower than those of whites in 1982; blacks' scores remain at this level, while there is a decline in the scores of whites, resulting in little difference between the two groups in 1983.

Such a pattern of change is also consistent with the model of labour market withdrawal outlined in the preceding section. It was suggested that changes in the level of job-seeking activity occur as a result of changes in job search attitude and expectations of getting a job. As people become more negative in their attitude towards looking for a job and more pessimistic about their chances of obtaining one, they tend to put less effort into looking for a job. The lower levels of job-seeking found among blacks in 1982, when compared with whites, can thus be explained by their lower scores on the job search attitude scale and their lower expectations of getting a job in the next six months. That is, one reason why blacks were putting less effort than whites into finding a job in 1982 may have been because blacks were less optimistic about their chances of finding a job and were more negative in their attitudes towards looking for work. However, this cannot be due to blacks having been unemployed for longer periods than whites, since there was no significant difference between the two groups in the length of their current unemployment spell or in the proportion of their time since leaving school spent unemployed. It is possible that black respondents' greater awareness of the difficulty of obtaining a job reflected a more general awareness of the disadvantages they faced due to discrimination in the labour market (Dex, 1979; Roberts et al. 1983). Yet although whites were more optimistic than blacks in 1982, and were trying harder to find a job, a further year of continuous unemployment was associated with a significant reduction in their expectations and a less positive attitude towards looking for work. Thus in 1983 whites were no more optimistic than blacks, and were no longer making greater efforts to find a job.

Table 7.3 shows that there were no marked differences between the sexes. Black and white females were similar in some respects, though in other ways they more closely resembled the males from their own ethnic group. With regard to the number of job applications made in the previous year, the number of job search methods used, and expectations of obtaining a job, both groups of females showed a greater decline than the corresponding groups of males (although the changes are not statistically significant among blacks). There were also falls in the level of females' employment commitment and an increase in their unemployment orientation. Although these changes were not statistically significant, they contrasted with the pattern found among males. Hence there was some evidence that females were becoming less committed to finding a job over the course of the two interviews, although the results from these longitudinal analyses do not show signs of a consistent pattern of change among both black and white females.

3. WITHDRAWAL FROM THE LABOUR MARKET

So far the approach we have adopted in addressing the "discouraged worker" hypothesis has been to look for patterns of change among selected variables. Thus we have highlighted the changes which accompany reductions in job-seeking activity over the course of the two interviews. In this way we have been able to interpret the meaning of reduced job-seeking, and the reasons which may lie behind such changes. The evidence we have presented suggests that young people do make less effort to find a job as their unemployment continues. By showing that this change is accompanied by changes in expectations of obtaining a job and in attitudes towards looking for work, we have supported the suggestion that it reflects a growing sense of discouragement rather than preference for unemployment. It appears that many young people 'scale down' their job hunting as they become more pessimistic about their chances of finding a job, but that they continue to desire employment and show little sign of growing to like being unemployed.

Such an approach focusses on the general patterns of change which are to be found among the sample as a whole. As such it cannot be expected to highlight those changes which might be occurring among specific sections within the sample. For example, there may be a number of females who withdraw from the labour market and adopt domestic roles. Such a group would not be revealed by analyses which are computed on the mean scores of all females. Similarly, by examining changes in the overall levels of job-seeking we have obscured differences which may have existed between those who were still active in job hunting (albeit at a reduced level) and those who were no longer looking for a job.

For reasons such as these, a second approach was used to investigate possible discouragement in our sample. In this we focussed our attention on those unemployed who, by 1983, reported that they were no longer looking for a job. Had these people given up looking for a job because they had become discouraged by successive failures to secure one? Or did they reject the idea of a work ethic, preferring the freedom of unemployment? By adopting such an approach we were also able to consider whether young women were more likely to stop looking for a job than were young men, and whether some blacks became so discouraged that they stopped looking for a job. In order to answer questions such as these it was

99

necessary to use longitudinal analyses. In this way we were able to examine the features which preceded withdrawal from job-seeking, and thus offer some tentative explanations of its occurrence. Hence all analyses were computed on those people who were interviewed both in 1982 and 1983 and who were unemployed on both occasions (n = 501).

Responses to the item measuring current job-seeking were used to identify those respondents who might be described as having withdrawn from the labour market. Hence respondents who reported in 1983 that they were "not really looking" for a job were classified as having withdrawn, while those responding in the other two categories ("I'm actively looking for a job" and "I'm keeping my eyes open but not looking hard") were classified as not having withdrawn. Such a classification is not perfect, and there may have been some overlap between these two categories. However, this can serve to strengthen confidence in any differences which are observed between the two groups.

A total of 92 respondents were classified by this method as having withdrawn from the labour market. This represented 18.4% of the unemployed longitudinal sample. The percentages among white males, black males, white females and black females were 7.4%, 13.3%, 31.3% and 25.0% respectively. Thus among males there was a higher proportion of blacks who had withdrawn than whites, while the reverse was true among females. Women from both ethnic groups were more likely to report they were not looking for a job than were their male counterparts. Chi-squared tests showed there was only one difference which was statistically significant, with white females being significantly more likely to report not looking for a job than were white males.

Comparisons between those not looking for a job and those who were looking were then made on a number of variables measured in 1983. These included some of the variables which have been discussed so far, as well as a number of additional variables which might also be associated with withdrawal. The latter include measures of the extent of financial worries (on a scale from 0 to 3, with a high score indicating fewer worries), ability to fill the time (scored 0 to 3, with a high score indicating greater ability), perceived difficulty of finding a job (on a scale from 1 to 4, with a high score indicating greater perceived difficulty), the proportion of the respondents' social contacts who were employed (scored from 1 to 3, with a high score indicating a higher proportion) and the reported level of concern over being unemployed (scored from 0 to 3, with a high score indicating greater concern).

Table 7.4 shows the mean scores on these variables for respondents who had withdrawn from seeking a job in 1983 and those who had not. Also shown in this table are the respective mean scores obtained in 1982, and the significance of the change from 1982 to 1983. These changes will be discussed in more detail below.

Not surprisingly, respondents who were not looking for a job in 1983 had significantly lower expectations of obtaining one in the following six months than had those who were still looking for work. The former also had a significantly lower level of employment commitment, a more positive unemployment orientation, and a less positive job search attitude. Those who reported looking for a job had made an average of almost one job application in the four weeks prior to being interviewed in 1983, while the figure was close to zero among those not looking for work. A similar difference was found in terms of the number of job search methods used during the same four week period. The low mean scores of those not looking for a job on these two job-seeking variables confirm that the majority were making little or no effort to find a job.

There was no significant difference between the two groups in terms of the difficulty they perceived in obtaining a job or in their degree of financial worries. However, those no longer looking for a job reported being more able to fill their time than did those still looking, and they spent their time with a significantly lower proportion of employed young people. They also reported less concern about being unemployed than did those who were looking for a job.

These analyses help to characterise the differences between those people who were not looking for a job when interviewed in 1983 and those who were. The former were less committed to obtaining paid employment, had a slightly more favourable attitude towards being unemployed, had a less positive attitude towards looking for work and were more pessimistic about their chances of finding a job in the coming six months. Hence in some respects they appear to have been more discouraged from seeking work, although they were also less likely to desire employment (as indicated by their lower employment commitment scores).

It is important to examine whether such differences existed between these two groups when they were first interviewed in 1982. Since about 70% of those not looking for a job in 1983 had reported in 1982 that they were actively looking for work or were 'keeping their eyes open' for a job, the majority of these people had given up looking for a job during the year that followed the first interview. Differences between the two groups in 1982 are therefore likely to have preceded withdrawal, and thus may explain why some withdrew from seeking a job and others did not. In contrast, differences between the two groups in 1983 which were not present in 1982 are more likely to be an outcome of withdrawal rather than a cause of it.

Table 7.4 shows that the differences in expectations and in job search attitude found in 1983 also existed between the two groups in 1982. Hence there are signs of discouragement

101

Table 7.4: Comparisons Between Withdrawn and Not Withdrawn at Time Two

| | | At Time 2 | | |
		Withdrawn	Not Withdrawn	p<
Employment commitment	t1	26.00	25.97	
	t2	23.50	25.84	0.001
	p<	0.001		
Unemployment orientation	t1	10.32	9.94	
	t2	11.22	10.06	0.05
	p<			
Disaffection with youth labour market	t1	20.49	19.79	
	t2	20.09	19.65	
	p<			
Job search attitude	t1	9.75	11.42	0.001
	t2	7.67	11.31	0.001
	p<	0.001		
Expectations of getting a job	t1	2.57	3.11	0.001
	t2	1.92	3.02	0.001
	p<	0.001		
Perceived difficulty of getting a job	t1	2.89	3.07	
	t2	3.00	3.07	
	p<			

Table 7.4 (cont.)

Lack of financial worries	t1	3.20	3.19
	t2	2.92	3.09
	p<		
Able to fill the time	t1	2.55	2.48
	t2	2.78	2.51
	p<	0.05	0.01
Unemployed contacts	t1	1.65	1.78
	t2	1.67	1.84
	p<		0.05
Concern with being unemployed	t1	1.30	1.57
	t2	0.97	1.54
	p<	0.01	0.05 / 0.001
Recent job applications	t1	0.88	1.25
	t2	0.11	0.98
	p<	0.001	0.01 / 0.001
Number of job search methods	t1	2.71	3.50
	t2	0.89	3.39
	p<	0.001	0.001 / 0.001

in 1982 among those who were found to be no longer looking for a job when interviewed in 1983. There were also significant declines in both of these variables for this group over the course of that year. There is thus some evidence to suggest that low expectations of obtaining a job and a negative attitude towards the utility of looking for work contributed to this group's withdrawal from job-seeking at the time of the second interview. If both of these variables imply discouragement, then there is also evidence that this sense of discouragement increased significantly over the year which followed the first interview.

The lower levels of employment commitment and the higher unemployment orientation scores which characterised those not looking for work in 1983 were not present in 1982. A reduction in the value placed on employment (perhaps indicating an increasing rejection of the work ethic) thus appears to be an outcome rather than a precursor, of the growing sense of discouragement which characterises those who had stopped looking for a job.

The perceived difficulty of obtaining a job, and financial worries, failed to distinguish between the two groups of respondents in 1982, as was also the case in 1983. Hence there is no evidence that those who had withdrawn from seeking work in 1983 lacked the financial incentive to obtain employment. The fact that both groups perceived the same amount of difficulty in obtaining a job in 1982 and in 1983, suggests that the greater optimism of those still looking for a job did not reflect a different view of the labour market. Both groups were aware of the difficulties they faced; those who stopped looking for work were simply less confident about their chances of overcoming these difficulties.

Among those not looking for work, their greater ability to fill the time, and the lower proportion of their social contacts who were employed, do not appear to have preceded their withdrawal from job-seeking. The two groups did not differ on these variables in 1982, although they did in 1983. It seems unlikely, therefore, that those people who had stopped looking for a job when interviewed in 1983 had done so because they were able to occupy their time doing other things, or because they had lots of friends who were also unemployed.

Table 7.4 also shows that those who were not looking for a job in 1983 reported being less concerned about being unemployed in 1982 than did those who were still looking for work. Withdrawal therefore seems to be more likely among those who are the least concerned about not having a job. Those who were found to be still looking for a job in 1983 tended to be more concerned in 1982, while there had been a further decline in the concern of those who had stopped looking in 1983.

Finally, Table 7.4 shows that the differences found between the two groups in 1983, in terms of the number of job applications made and job search methods used, were also present in 1982. The difference in 1982 was highly significant with regard to the number of job search methods used, but not so with regard to the number of job applications made. However, the trend is clear enough to suggest that the process of withdrawal had already begun by 1982, although it was to continue with significant declines in both of these variables in the year that followed.

Since some of the variables shown in Table 7.4 are intercorrelated, we cannot distinguish between those which are making a genuine contribution to a person's withdrawal from seeking work in 1983, and those which are simply reflecting the effects of other variables. For example, a negative attitude towards looking for a job may not itself contribute to a person's decision to stop looking for work. Instead it may reflect low expectations of obtaining employment, which in turn may be the major contributory factor in withdrawal from job-seeking. Multiple regression analyses allowed us to assess the independent contribution of each variable towards withdrawal in 1983, while controlling for the effects of other variables. We also included dummy variables representing the sex and ethnic group of respondents, so that we could assess the possible association with withdrawal of these two demographic variables. This also meant that any effects which were observed for other variables would be independent of sex and ethnic differences. The results of the multiple regression analyses are shown in Table 7.5.

Table 7.5 shows the variables measured in 1982 which were used as predictors of withdrawal in 1983. Respondents were given a score of 1 if they were still looking for a job, and a score of 2 if they were not; this was then used as the dependent variable. Asterisks mark those variables which significantly predicted withdrawal one year later. Four additional variables to those shown in Table 7.4 were included. The length of the current spell of unemployment when interviewed in 1982 was included to see if subsequent withdrawal was more likely among those unemployed for the longest periods. Another variable, continuous unemployment, indicated whether the respondent had been continuously unemployed since leaving school; this was also included as a potential predictor of withdrawal. The third new variable introduced was the educational qualifications of the respondent. There were three values of this variable: no qualifications, CSE passes only, and GCE 'O' level passes. The 1982 value of the variable which was used to designate withdrawal in 1983, namely current job-seeking, was the fourth new variable to be included for these analyses. By including this variable we could control for its possible effects on other variables. Hence we could be reasonably confident that

Table 7.5: Predicting Withdrawal at Time Two from Changes in Time One Variables

	Whole Sample	Males	Females
Time 1 values			
Sex	0.17***		
Ethnic group	0.00	-0.04	0.02
Length of unemployment	-0.08*	-0.11	-0.05
Educational qualifications	-0.03	-0.04	0.00
Employment commitment	0.05	-0.02	0.02
Unemployment orientation	0.01	0.06	0.02
Labour market disaffection	-0.03	-0.11	0.01
Job search attitude	-0.16**	-0.21*	-0.10
Expectations	-0.20***	-0.16*	-0.17*
Difficulty getting a job	-0.06	-0.03	-0.06
Concern with unemployment	0.01	-0.09	0.04
Lack of financial worries	-0.03	0.05	-0.12
Able to fill the time	0.01	0.10	0.09
Unemployed contacts	0.03	-0.04	0.06
Recent job applications	0.08	0.13	0.01
Current job seeking	0.11*	0.15*	0.07
Number of job search methods	-0.36***	-0.27**	-0.45***
Continuous unemployment	0.01	0.01	0.00

Table 7.5 (cont.)

Changes in

Employment commitment	0.09*	0.14*	0.10
Unemployment orientation	0.00	0.00	0.01
Labour market disaffection	0.04	0.11	-0.02
Job search attitude	0.16**	0.19*	0.09
Expectations	0.17***	0.04	0.21**
Difficulty getting a job	0.05	0.09	-0.01
Concern with unemployment	-0.03	0.10	-0.10
Lack of financial worries	0.08	-0.01	0.15*
Able to fill time	-0.01	0.06	-0.07
Unemployed contacts	0.01	0.12	-0.04
Recent job applications	-0.03	-0.06	-0.01
Number of job search methods	0.43***	0.27***	0.56***
Multiple R	0.64	0.50	0.74
Multiple R^2	0.41***	0.26***	0.55***

Note: * $p<0.05$, ** $p<0.01$, *** $p<0.001$

those variables which significantly predicted withdrawal in 1983 were not in fact reflecting differences in withdrawal which may have already existed in 1982.

Also included in the multiple regression analyses were the changes in scores, from 1982 to 1983, of most of these variables. This allowed us to see whether changes in certain variables, in addition to their 1982 values, were associated with withdrawal in 1983.

Table 7.5 shows the beta values for all of these variables, first for the whole sample and then for males and females separately. This is because sex proved to be a significant predictor of withdrawal, with females being more likely than males to have stopped looking for a job by 1983. No significant difference was found between blacks and whites in terms of their likelihood of withdrawing from seeking work.

The length of time a respondent had been unemployed when interviewed in 1982 significantly predicted whether or not they would be still looking for a job when interviewed in 1983. Perhaps surprisingly, the association was a negative one, with shorter spells of unemployment in 1982 being associated with a greater likelihood of withdrawal one year later. This does not contradict the model of labour withdrawal outlined above (see also Ullah and Banks 1985), since long spells of unemployment may still be leading to lower expectations, etc., which in turn may still determine withdrawal. It is possible that some other variable which has not been controlled for, and which is also correlated with length of unemployment, is accounting for this result. When analyses were computed for males and females separately, the contribution made by length of unemployment failed to be statistically significant.

The job search attitude of respondents in 1982 and their expectations of obtaining a job in the next six months both significantly predicted whether or not they had withdrawn from seeking a job one year later. This provides further support for the suggestion that discouragement, in the form of a negative attitude towards the value of looking for work and low expectations of success, was a significant contributory factor in a person's decision to stop looking for a job.

Expectations of obtaining a job remained a significant predictor of withdrawal when analyses were computed for males and females separately, although job search attitude was significant only among males. Moreover, the lower section of Table 7.5 shows that a decline in scores on the job search attitude scale also significantly predicted withdrawal, but that once again this was the case only among males. In contrast, a decline in expectations of obtaining a job significantly predicted withdrawal, but only among females. Hence withdrawal from seeking a job was associated with a decline in job search attitude among males, and a decline in expectations among females. While the pattern of change among males is consistent with the discouragement hypothesis, the pattern of change among females may reflect a different reason for having stopped looking for a job. Young women who decide to pursue an alternative to employment, perhaps raising a family or looking after a home, will see this as occupying their time for the foreseeable future. Their low expectations of having a job in six months time may therefore reflect, rather than be a reason for, their decision not to look for a job.

Two other variables measured in 1982 significantly predicted withdrawal one year later (see Table 7.5). Current job-seeking, which was used to indicate withdrawal in 1983, was a significant predictor of this one year earlier. However, this was only the case among males. This suggests that less change occured among males, since it implies that those who reported low levels of current job-seeking in 1982 were likely to have withdrawn from seeking a job in 1983. In contrast, females appear less consistent, with those reporting high levels of current job-seeking in 1982 being just as likely to withdraw as those reporting low levels. The remaining variable predicting withdrawal was the number of job search methods used in the four weeks prior to the interview in 1982. Those people who were using the fewest number of ways of looking for a job were most likely to have stopped looking by 1983. Withdrawal was also significantly associated with a decline in the number of methods used, as shown in the lower half of Table 7.5. Those people who had stopped looking for a job when interviewed in 1983 were therefore likely to have been making less effort to find a job in 1982 than were those who were to remain in the labour market, and declined even further in their efforts as the year progressed. This pattern was found to be similar for both males and females.

4.   VARIABLES PREDICTING SUCCESS IN OBTAINING A JOB

In this chapter we have been concerned with the possible existence of discouragement among the long term unemployed in our sample. We have also focussed on those who, by 1983, had stopped looking for a job, and we have examined the possible reasons for their withdrawal from the labour market. Having identified some of the psychological processes involved, we believe it is necessary to go beyond the act of explanation and to look further ahead into the lives of these individuals. In particular, we need to inquire into some of the consequences of a reduction in or withdrawal from seeking employment. In Chapter 8 we will be looking at the relationship between the unemployed person's commitment to finding a job and their level of psychological well-being. In the remainder of the present chapter we will consider the effect a low level of job-seeking is likely to have on a person's chances of finding a job in the relatively near future.

At first sight this may seem an unproblematic, and even trivial, issue. Those people in our sample who were putting little or no effort into finding a job were undoubtedly unlikely to obtain one, given the high youth unemployment rates at the time of our study. However, were they any less likely to obtain a job than were those who were making considerably more effort? The growing sense of discouragement observed among those unemployed for the longest periods was, we have suggested, a reaction to repeated failure to secure a job. Does it make any difference then, in terms of job prospects, if poorly qualified unemployed young people keep on trying to find a job? Or are they just as likely to remain unemployed as are those who have given up, at least for the time being, looking for employment?

We investigated this issue by seeing if there was a significant association between the level of job seeking activity of the unemployed in 1982 and whether or not they managed to obtain a job in the year that followed. If no significant association was found it would suggest that those who were making more effort to find a job were just as likely to remain unemployed as were those who were making less effort.

This type of approach also allowed us to address a number of related issues. For instance, were those who were most positive in their attitudes towards seeking and obtaining employment more likely to be successful than those who were less positive? Young unemployed people are also encouraged not to be too fussy about the kind of work they accept, or to be prepared to work for relatively low rates of pay. But does lowering their aspirations in this way increase their chances of obtaining a job? Such motivational variables also need to be compared with those variables which are outside the personal control of the unemployed. For example, the colour of a person's skin, or whether they are male or female, may exert a far greater influence on their future chances of employment than does their level of commitment and effort.

These issues were explored using the longitudinal data set. Those people who were re-interviewed in 1983 were divided into those who had obtained a job since the first interview in 1982 (n = 257, including those who had subsequently lost this job by 1983) and those who had not obtained a job (n = 475). Comparisons between these two groups were then made on a number of variables measured at the time of the first interview. The results of t-tests are shown in Table 7.6.

There were a number of significant difference in 1982 between those who were to get a job in the year that followed and those who were to remain unemployed. Those who went on to get jobs had been making significantly more job applications

Table 7.6: Comparisons Between Respondents Obtaining and Not Obtaining Jobs

	Obtain a Job	Not Obtain Job	p<
1982 variables (mean scores)			
Number of job applications since leaving school	4.13	3.47	0.001
Number of job search methods	4.30	3.25	0.001
Take any job	1.47	1.39	
Lowest starting pay	34.37	34.67	
Expectations of getting a job	3.31	3.00	0.001
Current job seeking	2.56	2.30	0.001
Difficulty of obtaining a job	3.09	3.06	
Employment commitment	26.84	25.95	0.05
Unemployment orientation	9.36	10.13	0.05
Disaffection with youth labour market	18.88	20.15	0.001
Job search attitude	12.43	11.00	0.001
Educational qualifications	1.81	1.57	0.001
Local unemployment rate ranking	5.18	6.44	0.001
Length of current unemployment	21.57	27.16	0.001

111

since they left school, they reported using more varied methods of looking for work, had higher expectations of obtaining a job, and their own reports of their current level of job-seeking were higher than the reports of those who failed to get jobs. Significant differences were also found on all four of the labour market attitude scales. Those who later obtained jobs had, in 1982, a significantly higher level of employment commitment, a lower unemployment orientation, a more positive job search attitude, and were less disaffected than those who remained unemployed.

During the interviews respondents were also asked if they would accept any job they were offered (Yes, No, scored 2 and 1 respectively), and to state the lowest level of starting pay they were prepared to accept. No significant differences, on these two variables were found between those who later obtained jobs and those who did not. The differences in the difficulty they perceived in obtaining a job also proved to be non-significant.

Respondents were also compared in terms of the length of their current unemployment spell in 1982, and their level of educational qualifications. Although one of our sampling requirements was that no-one should have more than two GCE 'O' levels, in these analyses we distinguished between those who possessed up to two 'O' levels, those who possessed only CSE passes, and those with no qualifications (scored 3, 2, 1 respectively). We also ranked the eleven sampling sites according to their unemployment rates for August 1982, with the area with the lowest rate being ranked first, and so on. This provided us with a variable which reflected the possible effects of local unemployment levels. Table 7.6 shows that those people in 1982 who were to obtain a job in the following year had been unemployed for a shorter period of time, had a higher level of educational qualifications, and lived in areas of lower unemployment rates than did those who failed to obtain jobs.

Sex and ethnic comparisons (not shown in Table 7.6) showed that among males there was a significant ($p < 0.001$) association between the ethnic group of the respondent and whether or not they obtained a job between 1982 and 1983. Only 17.2% of black males obtained jobs compared with 42.9% of white males. Although the association was not significant among females in the sample, only 27.4% of black females obtained jobs, compared with 40.2% of white females. No significant sex differences, among blacks or whites, were found between the proportions obtaining a job.

These results point to a number of variables which may influence a person's chances of obtaining a job. Those respondents who, in 1982, were most active in looking for work, those who had the most positive labour market attitudes, and those with the highest qualifications were most likely to obtain a job in the year that followed.

Black respondents (when compared with whites) and those living in areas of relatively high unemployment rates, were less likely to obtain jobs. Being prepared to accept any job, or to work for lower rates of pay, were not significantly associated with subsequent success in finding a job. In addition to this we also compared those who obtained but then lost jobs by the time of our second interview, with those who were still in employment at that time. No significant differences were found on any of the variables considered here, except for local unemployment rate. Those who were to lose their jobs lived in an area with a lower unemployment rate ranking (indicating higher local unemployment rates). Our decision to combine these two groups for the analyses shown in Table 7.6 is therefore justified, since they do not appear to differ on the key psychological variables.

We then used multiple regression analyses to assess the independent contributions of each of these variables towards predicting success in finding a job. This is important since some of the variables shown in Table 7.6 are likely to be intercorrelated. For example, the association between greater job-seeking activity and subsequent success in finding a job may simply reflect the possibility that those people making the most job applications were living in areas where unemployment rates were low and where job vacancies were more plentiful. Thus their success may be an effect of the latter, rather than simple effort. Similarly, it is important to consider the possible causes of the observed ethnic differences in success in finding a job. For example, were black respondents less likely to obtain a job because they were not looking for one as hard as were whites, or did ethnic differences persist after controlling for the level of job-seeking activity?

Table 7.7 shows the results of the multiple regression analyses. Included among the predictor variables are dummy variables representing three types of employment history during the year prior to the initial interview in 1982: (i) previous experience of employment; (ii) previous experience of YOP; (iii) previous experience of employment and YOP. These variables are coded such that the beta value for each represents the extent to which individuals experiencing that particular kind of history were more likely to obtain a job than were those who had been continuously unemployed since leaving school.

Predictor variables were introduced into the analysis in four separate stages. The first stage consisted of those variables reflecting the attitudinal orientation of the unemployed to the labour market, and their level of educational attainment. In contrast to Table 7.6, only two of these variables retained a significant independent association with future success in obtaining a job. Respondents with a more positive job search attitude, and those with a higher

113

Table 7.7: Variables Predicting Future Success in Obtaining Employment (significances as Table 7.5)
(* p<0.05, ** p<0.01, *** p<0.001)

Variable (1982)	Stage			
	1	2	3	4
Take any job	-0.04	-0.03	-0.02	-0.02
Lowest starting pay	0.01	0.00	-0.01	-0.03
Job expectations	0.06	0.04	0.02	0.01
Educational qualifications	0.11**	0.07*	0.08*	0.08*
Difficulty of obtaining a job	0.02	-0.01	-0.01	-0.01
Employment commitment	0.01	0.00	0.02	0.01
Unemployment orientation	-0.03	0.01	0.01	0.00
Disaffection with youth labour market	-0.07	-0.07	-0.07	-0.05
Job search attitude	0.17***	0.08	0.07	0.07
Current job seeking		0.01	0.01	0.00
Number of job applications since leaving school		0.11**	0.09*	0.08*
Number of job search methods		0.18***	0.15**	0.15***
Sex			-0.01	0.00
Ethnic group			-0.15***	-0.14***
Previous job(s)			0.13**	0.11**
Previous YOP(s)			0.07	0.08
Previous job(s) and YOP(s)			0.09*	0.09*
Local unemployment rate ranking				-0.13***
R^2	0.07***	0.12***	0.15***	0.17***

114

level of educational qualifications, were significantly more likely to obtain a job in the year that followed.

At the second stage, the three reports of job-seeking activity were included as predictor variables. The number of job applications made in the previous year, and the number of job search methods used in the four weeks prior to our interviews, were both positively associated with obtaining a job in the year that followed. Educational qualifications remained significant, although there was a fall in the level of significance. Job search attitude was no longer a significant predictor variable, suggesting that its initial effect was due to its association with the job-seeking variables.

The sex and ethnicity of respondents were included as predictor variables in the third stage, along with the type of employment history experienced since leaving school. No significant association was found between the sex of the respondent and subsequent success in obtaining a job, although whites in 1982 were significantly more likely to obtain a job in the following year than were blacks. Since the effects of other predictor variables are being controlled for in these analyses, this difference is independent of any other differences between blacks and whites in terms of educational qualifications, number of job applications made, employment commitment, and so on.

In comparison with those people who had been continuously unemployed since leaving school, those who had had a job were significantly more likely to obtain another job in the year that followed, as were those who had experience of employment and YOP. However, those who had experience only of YOP were no more likely to obtain a job.

In the fourth stage of analysis, the variable based on the ranking of the eleven sampling sites in terms of their local unemployment rate was added to the equation. This was significantly associated with subsequent success in obtaining a job, with respondents living in the areas of higher unemployment being less likely to obtain a job. Once again this effect was independent of how hard people in those areas were trying to get a job, their educational qualifications, and so on. At this final stage, with all predictor variables included in the equation, educational qualifications, number of job applications, number of job search methods, previous experience of employment, and ethnic group remained significant predictors of future success in obtaining a job.

These analyses show that greater job-seeking efforts do result in an increased likelihood of obtaining a job. Conversely, this implies that those who become discouraged from looking for a job are even less likely to obtain one, thus perpetuating their unemployment and placing them in a vicious circle. Educational qualifications, even within the limited range held by members of our sample, do increase their chances of obtaining a job. However, being prepared to accept any job or to work for low rates of pay do not significantly increase these chances. Black respondents, and those who live in those sampling areas with the highest local unemployment rates, were significantly less likely to obtain jobs in the following year. Thus although there are some things which the unemployed can do to increase their chances of finding a job, there are other influences outside their control which act as obstacles to this. Furthermore, those who have no experience of employment are likely to find this a factor in their future inability to obtain a job and preventing them from gaining the necessary experience.

CONCLUSION

In this chapter we have examined the relationship between unemployment, various labour market attitudes, and the motivation to seek employment. There are many assumptions about the nature of this relationship among young people, ranging from views that the young prefer life on the dole (and thus are likely to remain unemployed unless it is made less attractive), to the view that many have become totally discouraged about ever being able to obtain a job. We have attempted to provide empirical data relating to these issues, so that the debate may be informed by factual evidence. The analyses we have used have been complex, and we have adopted various approaches. Yet these are complex issues, and so demand comprehensive examination. One of the limitations of previous research into the attitudes and values of the young unemployed is that it has often failed to be comprehensive. Cross-sectional designs have been used where longitudinal studies would have been more appropriate; or the range of variables considered has not been adequate to explore the different facets of the motivation to seek work. Given the detailed and the lengthy nature of this chapter, a brief summary of the main findings should serve to clarify how we see these issues as they relate to young, poorly qualified unemployed people.

The first part of the chapter was concerned with the attitudes of the unemployed towards both employment and unemployment. Although it has been suggested that there has been a decline in the work ethic, particularly over the last fifty years, studies of young people suggest that the vast majority are committed to obtaining paid employment. More importantly, the primary motivation to secure employment does not appear to be financial. Most young people in these studies said that they would continue to work if it was no longer financially necessary to do so. This finding was reproduced in our own data, with over three-quarters of the unemployed people interviewed in 1983 echoing this sentiment.

Hence our results are consistent with those reported by Warr (1982), Feather and Davenport (1981), Feather and Bond (1983), Jackson et al. (1983), and Tiggemann and Winefield (1980) in failing to support the notion that the majority of young unemployed people do not want to have a job.

Our own study went further than measuring commitment to employment, and also obtained measures of the extent of favourable attitudes towards unemployment. Once again we found little to suggest that young people in our sample actually enjoyed being without a job. Even those who felt that there were certain advantages to being unemployed, mostly in terms of the greater freedom of time it entailed, still displayed significantly higher levels of psychological distress than the employed people we interviewed. Taken together, our findings on attitudes towards employment and unemployment show that the vast majority of the unemployed people in our sample strongly desired a job and viewed unemployment in extremely negative terms.

In the latter part of this chapter we took the question of the motivation to seek work one step further. Given that most unemployed people in our sample disliked being without a job and wished that they could obtain one, was it nevertheless the case that they had become so discouraged that they were no longer making any effort to find a job? Several approaches were adopted in investigating this issue. Cross-sectional analyses confirmed that the longer a person had been unemployed, the less effort he or she was putting into job hunting. However, those unemployed for the longest periods did not have lower levels of employment commitment or a more favourable unemployment orientation. Their lower levels of job-seeking were thus unlikely to reflect a lack of desire for employment or an attachment to unemployment. Rather, they appeared to reflect pessimism about the chances of obtaining a job. Increasing periods of unemployment were associated with increasingly negative attitudes towards looking for a job and lower expectations about the possibility of obtaining one. This suggests that, for some people in our sample, continuing unemployment was associated with an increasing sense of discouragement and a corresponding reduction in the effort they were making to find a job.

These results are consistent with those reported by Feather (1982) and Feather and Barber (1983), who found no association in their respective samples between the length of time spent unemployed and the value attached to employment. Our own findings are also consistent with the negative correlation between length of unemployment and level of job-seeking reported by Feather (1982).

Longitudinal analyses confirmed there had been an actual decline in scores on selected variables among those people continuously unemployed between 1982 and 1983. Levels of job-seeking fell significantly during this period, as did

117

expectations and positive attitudes towards looking for a job, while there was no change in employment commitment and unemployment orientation. Disaffection with the youth labour market appeared to increase with up to a year of continuous unemployment and then 'level off' at this high value. These longitudinal analyses support Feather and Davenport's (1981) expectancy-valence model of job-seeking: namely, that prolonged unemployment leads to decreased expectations and a reduction in the motivation to seek employment.

A second approach adopted here was to focus on those people who, in 1983, reported that they were no longer seeking a job. We were thus able to see if they displayed the characteristics of discouragement, and whether there were any other possible reasons for such withdrawal from the labour market. Kelvin and Jarrett (1985) have recently criticised those approaches to the study of youth unemployment which provide case studies of young people already discouraged, since "we need to know what they were like, and how they acted, before they became discouraged" (p.38). We were able to meet this need by examining the characteristics in 1982 of those not seeking employment in 1983.

Our analyses strongly suggest that discouragement was a major reason behind the decision of many of our sample to withdraw from seeking employment. Those who, in 1982, had low expectations of obtaining a job in the next six months and who viewed job-seeking as unlikely to result in success, were significantly more likely to have stopped looking for a job one year later than were those with higher expectations and more positive attitudes towards job-seeking. In this respect our data support Hesketh and Shouksmith's (1982) warning that if the young unemployed do not remain optimistic then they may give up looking for a job.

Our data failed to support alternative reasons which have been suggested for young people not making the effort to find a job. Those who had withdrawn from job-seeking in 1983 had not previously, in 1982, expressed more favourable attitudes towards being unemployed or possessed a lower level of employment commitment than those who were still looking in 1983. Neither did they lack the financial incentive for a job, since in 1982 they reported financial worries as equally serious as those who were to remain in the labour market. Hence we found no evidence to suggest that the people in our sample who withdrew from the labour market did so because they no longer wanted a job, or because they enjoyed being unemployed or were getting enough money on the dole.

Our analysis of the differences between these two groups in 1983 which were not present in 1982 also suggested some of the features which may be an outcome of the decision to withdraw from the labour market. There were signs that a lower level of employment commitment and a more favourable unemployment orientation, although not contributors to the decision to withdraw, were likely to follow from this decision. Hence the rejection of the work ethic much feared by politicians and policy-makers may in fact occur if young people become so discouraged from looking for a job that they decide to no longer bother to do so. Similarly, there were signs that, having stopped looking for a job, the people in our sample were filling their time in other ways and were spending more time with other unemployed young people. There is thus some justification for the concern of the Manpower Services Commission (1981b) with the possibility of there developing "concentrations of unemployed and possibly disaffected young people" (p.26).

We were also able to pinpoint sex and ethnic differences in some of these patterns of behaviour. In 1982 we found that unemployed blacks in our sample were making fewer job applications and using fewer ways of looking for work than were unemployed whites. It is possible that this reflected greater pessimism on the part of young blacks. At that time blacks' expectations of obtaining a job were much lower than those of whites, and they placed less faith in job-seeking. Yet none of these differences were present one year later. Our longitudinal analyses, computed on only those who had been continuously unemployed between the two interviews, strongly suggested that during the course of a further year's unemployment whites had grown to be as pessimistic as blacks.

The greater pessimism among blacks in 1982 could not be attributed to their having experienced more unemployment, since in this respect they did not differ from whites (see Chapter 5). One possible explanation is that a life of disadvantage, arising out of being black in Britain today, had better prepared them for the grim realities of the youth labour market. When they were interviewed one year after leaving school, many appeared to be aware of their limited chances of success. Whites, on the other hand, required a further year of unemployment before they too reflected the same degree of pessimism. Such an interpretation is supported by unstructured interviews conducted with young black people (Ullah, 1987). Many of these people were acutely aware of the obstacles they had faced in life due to being black, and viewed their future in extremely pessimistic terms. Yet they believed themselves to be better equipped than whites for coping with such disadvantage, having had more experience of it.

The growing sense of discouragement, which we would argue accounts for some of the reasons for withdrawing from the labour market, thus appears to have applied to both black and whites in our sample. The two ethnic groups differed however, in the time-scale over which this process occurred. This pattern was not present in the sex differences which were found within the sample. Females were more likely to withdraw from seeking a job than were males, and appeared to do so for quite different reasons. Although low expectations of obtaining a job appeared to be a contributory factor in the decision of both males and females to stop looking, a negative attitude towards actually looking for a job was an additional factor among males only. Moreover, job search attitude did not become increasingly more negative from 1982 to 1983 among females, as it did among males. Males who withdrew from job-seeking, then, appeared to do so because they had become discouraged. In contrast, the low expectations of obtaining a job which preceded withdrawal among females may be more indicative of a change of plans for their future. Those women in the sample who planned to withdraw from the labour market in the near future, perhaps because of domestic or childcaring responsibilities, would be likely to report low expectations of having a job at that time. Those women who intended to marry in the following year may also have planned to withdraw from job-seeking, since the current state benefit system discourages the wives of unemployed men from obtaining employment. Whatever the reason for planning to stop looking for a job in the near future, it is likely to be reflected in reports of low expectations of having a job in six months' time, and thus explain why this alone predicted withdrawal among females in the sample.

Chapter 8

GOOD AND POOR COPERS: VARIATIONS IN THE EXPERIENCE OF
UNEMPLOYMENT

In Chapter 6 we showed that the levels of psychological well-
being among the unemployed in our sample were significantly
lower than the levels found among those who, in 1983, were
employed. These comparisons were based on the overall mean
scores on our three principal well-being measures. Yet around
any mean score there is usually some variation, and the
purpose of this chapter is to explore the meaning of the
variation that was found in the unemployed sample.   In
particular, we will be looking at the attitudes, experiences
and patterns of behaviour that tend to be associated with
relatively good mental health during unemployment, and those
that tend to be associated with poor mental health.   We will
be asking: who are the good copers, and who are the poor
copers? Such an investigation is essential if we are to offer
constructive advice on how to make the experience of
unemployment more bearable for young people, and conversely,
how to prevent it from becoming unbearable.
        Discussion in this chapter will be grouped around three
central issues relating to this aim. The first relates to the
question of commitment discussed in the previous chapter, and
we will consider whether greater commitment to finding a job
causes greater distress during unemployment. The second issue
is the possible role played by the friends, family and other
social contacts of the unemployed person, both in supporting
them and in creating additional problems. Finally, we will
look at the ways in which the unemployed in our sample were
spending their time. We will consider how far their level of
psychological well-being could be attributed to how well they
were managing to fill the gap left by not having a job.

1.   EMPLOYMENT COMMITMENT AND PSYCHOLOGICAL WELL-BEING

Several studies, using measures of employment commitment
similar or identical to our own, have shown that those
unemployed people who most strongly desire employment tend to

experience greater psychological distress than those who less strongly desire employment. Thus significant positive correlations between employment commitment scores and GHQ scores have been reported by Stafford et al. (1980), Warr and Jackson (1983, 1985) and Jackson et al. (1983). Some of these studies have also shown that those people with high employment commitment tend to exhibit a deterioration in their psychological well-being as their period of unemployment continues, that this effect is independent of other factors such as financial strain (Warr and Jackson, 1985), and that the level of commitment remains fairly stable as people move in and out of employment (Jackson et al., 1983). However, for employed people, greater employment commitment tends to be associated with less psychological distress (Stafford et al. 1980).

Employment commitment has therefore been described as a relatively stable attribute which tends to moderate the psychological impact of unemployment (Fryer and Payne, 1986). People who are very committed to having paid employment tend to have relatively high levels of psychological well-being when they are employed but relatively low levels when they are unemployed.

Although it is hardly surprising that lower psychological well-being is found among those unemployed people who most strongly desire a job, the precise psychological processes involved need to be specified. One possible explanation has been suggested by Feather and his colleagues (Feather and Davenport, 1981; Feather and Barber, 1983). They describe a "frustrated work motivation pattern" which may account for the observed relationship between psychological well-being and the importance attached to having a job. Drawing upon expectancy-valence theory (Feather, 1982) they suggest that the motivation to seek employment when unemployed is partly related to the value placed on having a job and partly related to the expectations of obtaining one. Thus, greater efforts to find a job will be made by those people who most value employment as a goal and/or those who most expect their efforts to result in success. However, when those efforts prove to be unsuccessful, the effect is one of greater disappointment and sadness than would be the case had employment not been so strongly desired and/or expected. It is suggested that this disappointment will be reflected in greater depressive affect.

This analysis suggests that those unemployed people who most value employment tend to exhibit poor psychological well-being because they are likely to have made the most effort to find a job and also to have experienced the most disappointment from their failure. Support for this is provided by Feather and Davenport (1981), who found that within a sample of unemployed young people, those who reported the most depressive affect tended to be those who most valued employment, those who left school with the highest expectations of obtaining a job, and those who were making the most effort to find a job.

The relationship between psychological well-being and both the value placed on obtaining a job (employment commitment) and the effort put into finding one, may enable us to identify those people in our sample who were most able to cope with their unemployment and those who were least able to cope. The relationship suggests that those unemployed people for whom employment is not such a salient goal, perhaps because they have come to aim for alternative goals, may be experiencing less distress than those for whom employment is more important. Evidence supporting this has been reported by Warr et al. (1982). Amongst one cohort of females in their sample, longer spells of unemployment were associated with lower levels of employment commitment and, correspondingly, lower levels of psychological distress. The authors suggest that the relatively low employment commitment scores reflected the fact that many of those women were either pregnant or were caring for a child and so no longer viewed employment as a salient goal.

It is also possible that some people cope with unemployment by reducing the amount of effort they put into finding a job. In the previous chapter we showed that, in our sample, a reduction in effort was not necessarily accompanied by a fall in employment commitment. These people still desired a job but, due to successive failures, had grown discouraged from looking for one. Yet the analysis provided by Feather and Davenport (1981) suggests that their reduced effort, even if not accompanied by reduced employment commitment, may be associated with better psychological well-being. Although many studies have examined the association between employment commitment and psychological well-being, there have been none which have considered the relationship between well-being and a range of job-seeking behaviours and labour market attitudes such as the range which was obtained from our sample of young people.

These associations, for all respondents unemployed in 1983, are shown in Table 8.1. As with other studies, employment commitment was significantly correlated with GHQ scores. It was also correlated with our measures of depression and anxiety. There is clear evidence, then, that those people in our unemployed sample who were most committed to obtaining paid employment were experiencing poorer psychological health. Conversely, unemployment orientation, measuring favourable attitudes towards being unemployed, was negatively correlated with our three measures of well-being. So those people who were able to view positive aspects to their unemployment tended to be coping relatively well, in terms of their psychological well-being.

Table 8.1: Correlations of Labour Market Attitudes and Job-Seeking Activities with Measures of Psychological Well-Being

	GHQ	Depression	Anxiety
Employment commitment	0.26	0.28	0.26
Unemployment orientation	-0.21	-0.28	-0.15
Disaffection with youth labour market	0.18	0.17	0.15
Job search attitudes	0.00	0.01	-0.02
Job expectations	-0.07	-0.06	-0.05
Job applications in last year	0.11	0.09	0.08
Number of job search methods	0.13	0.10	0.10
Current job seeking	0.04	0.04	-0.03

Note: n = 1054, p<0.05 when r = 0.06, p<0.01 when r = 0.08, p<0.001 when r = 0.09

Of the two remaining labour market attitudes that we measured, disaffection with the youth labour market and job search attitude, only the former was significantly associated with well-being levels. Higher levels of disaffection were associated with higher GHQ, depression and anxiety scores. A generally negative and cynical attitude towards opportunities in the youth labour market and agencies such as the Careers Service, therefore, tended to be accompanied by poorer psychological well-being. However job search attitude, which measures attitudes towards looking for a job, was unrelated to well-being levels.

A weak association (p<0.05) was found between expectations of obtaining a job in the next six months and GHQ and depression scores. The tendency was for higher expectations to be accompanied by lower levels of distress (GHQ) and depression, although such small correlation coefficients are unlikely to be reliable. Optimism about future job prospects, then, does not provide a strong indication of good psychological well-being. One reason for this may be that high expectations were also associated with greater job-seeking efforts, and Table 8.1 shows that the number of job applications made in the previous year, and the number of job seeking methods used in the previous four weeks, were both significantly correlated with all three well-being measures. Those people who were making the most effort to find a job were experiencing higher levels of distress, depression and anxiety. Respondents' own reports of their level of current job seeking, however, were unrelated to the three well-being measures.

In the previous chapter we described how there was a tendency for those people who had been unemployed for the longest periods to be putting less effort into finding a job. This reduction in job seeking did not reflect a lack of desire to have a job, since the employment commitment scores of these people were just as high as the scores of those recently unemployed. Instead it appeared to reflect a growing sense of discouragement, since it was accompanied by low expectations of obtaining a job and a negative attitude towards looking for one. The analyses we have presented here suggest that this form of gradual withdrawal from the labour market may have implications for the psychological well-being of the person concerned. In particular, our results suggest that it may be accompanied by improvements in well-being, since lower levels of job-seeking tended to be associated with lower GHQ, depression and anxiety scores. It is plausible to suggest, therefore, that reductions in the level of job-seeking reflected not only discouragement but also an awareness of the distress caused by continually seeking jobs when there is little chance of success. A withdrawal from this latter position may thus represent a conscious strategy of coping with unemployment.

Such an interpretation allows us to suggest an explanation for the pattern of ethnic differences observed in our measures of psychological well-being. The higher GHQ and depression scores found among whites when compared with blacks in 1982 partly reflected the greater efforts of whites to find a job at that time (Warr, Banks and Ullah, 1985). The significant reduction in effort found among those whites who remained unemployed up to our second interview in 1983 (see Chapter 7) may therefore account for the absence of any ethnic differences in well-being scores in 1983 (Banks and Ullah, 1986).

If 'scaling down' job-seeking efforts is a way of coping with unemployment, then it appears to be a strategy which blacks are quicker than whites to learn. After just one year in the labour market blacks in our sample were making less effort to find a job than were whites, and were experiencing fewer psychological symptoms. It required a further year of unemployment before whites reduced their efforts to the level of blacks and displayed similar levels of well-being.

2. SOCIAL SUPPORTS, SOCIAL CONTACTS AND SOCIAL PRESSURES

There is considerable evidence from clinical studies that the presence of supportive social relationships can lessen the psychological ill-health which typically follows a period of great stress. Thus in coping with major life events such as bereavement, people tend to cope better if they can turn to others for emotional and practical support (Brown and Harris, 1978; Caplan, 1974; Cassel, 1976; Cobb, 1976).

Given this fact it seems reasonable to assume that those unemployed young people in our sample who could rely on support from others may have been coping relatively well with the experience of being unemployed. In contrast, those who lacked support may have been among the poor copers in our sample.

Although it has often been suggested that social support may moderate the harmful psychological effects of unemployment (Hayes and Nutman, 1981; Kaufman, 1982; Warr, 1984a and b), there have been relatively few attempts to test this empirically. Gore (1978) has described a longitudinal study in which employees at two factories in the U.S. were interviewed before and after closure of their plant. Those respondents who scored low on a scale of social support reported a greater number of illness symptoms than those who scored high on this scale, both before and after job loss. However, it is not possible to tell from Gore's presentation of the data whether unsupported people also had higher levels of depression. The comparisons were also based on very small samples (15 and 33). There is, then, a need for the possible beneficial effects of social support to be assessed on a range of psychological well-being measures and for much larger samples of unemployed people, such as our own sample.

In our study we examined various kinds of social support. We asked unemployed respondents to indicate whether they had someone to turn to for help with money, someone to talk with about day-to-day problems, someone who could suggest interesting things to do, someone to turn to for cheering up when feeling low, and someone to provide information about jobs and benefits. In this way we were able to follow the suggestion that a distinction be made between emotional and instrumental forms of social support (Thoits, 1982). In 1982 when all respondents in our initial sample were unemployed we found that the proportions reporting these forms of support ranged from 51% (having someone to suggest interesting things to do) to 86% (having someone to turn to for help with money).

We then examined the association between each form of support and our principal well-being measures. Did those unemployed respondents who possessed some form of social support have higher levels of well-being than those who did not possess such support? The findings from our 1982 sample have since been published (Ullah, Banks and Warr, 1985) and are reproduced here in Table 8.2. This table shows the simple correlations between each social support item and our measures of distress (GHQ), depression and anxiety.

Despite significant inter-correlations between the support items, only two of the five were found to be significantly associated with the well-being measures. Those people who had someone to turn to for help with money, and those who had someone to turn to for suggestions about interesting things to do, had significantly lower GHQ, depression and anxiety scores than those not possessing these respective forms of support. When we examined the mean well-being scores of supported and unsupported people we found that the former had lower GHQ, depression and anxiety scores than those of the sample as a whole, while unsupported people had scores which were considerably higher than those of the whole sample.

There were signs, then, that those people who possessed either of these practical forms of support tended to be coping relatively well with their period of unemployment. Those who lacked either form of support tended to be coping relatively poorly. However, no significant difference was found between those who possessed, and those who did not possess, the other three kinds of support. It is possible that boredom and lack of money are two features of unemployment which are particularly hard to bear for young people. Support in either respect may therefore be more beneficial to their psychological well-being than the other forms of support that we measured.

We also looked for possible sex and ethnic differences in the relationship between social support and mental health. We

Table 8.2: Correlations Among Social Support Items with Measures of Psychological Well-Being

	Support Items				
	1	2	3	4	5
Support					
1. Help with money					
2. Talk about day-to-day problems	0.19***				
3. Suggest interesting things to do	0.15***	0.23***			
4. Cheering up when feeling low	0.15***	0.30***	0.26***		
5. Information on jobs and benefits	0.06	0.16***	0.19***	0.12***	
Psychological well-being					
GHQ	-0.16***	0.00	-0.14***	0.00	-0.03
Depression	-0.17***	-0.05	-0.15***	-0.03	-0.06
Anxiety	-0.10***	0.00	-0.08**	0.00	-0.01

Note: n = 1,150, **p<0.01 ***p<0.001

found that not having someone to suggest interesting things to do was more detrimental to the well-being of females and whites than it was to males and blacks, respectively. Also, females who reported not having someone to cheer them up when feeling low had lower levels of psychological well-being than those who possessed this form of support, though there was no such difference among males. Some forms of support, then, appear to have been more important for females than for males. Similarly, blacks did not appear to suffer as much as did whites from not having someone to suggest interesting things to do.

Another issue which was investigated was that of the amount of contact with other young people reported by the unemployed in our sample. Several writers have suggested that unemployment is associated with an increase in social isolation (e.g. Coffield et al., 1983; Eisenberg and Lazarsfeld, 1938; O'Brien and Kabanoff, 1979). However, Roberts et al., (1982a) have stated that among young people "unemployment is rarely socially isolating or experienced as a stigma" (p.2). Similarly, Warr (1984c) has reported finding a significant increase in contacts with friends after job loss among adults, especially those under 25 years of age. We were particularly keen to see whether the amount of social contact reported by the people in our sample was associated with their level of psychological well-being. Were those who reported social isolation experiencing poorer psychological health than those who were not socially isolated from their peer group?

Related to this question is the possible effect on well-being of having other unemployed people among one's social contacts. It has been suggested that people who live in areas of high unemployment feel less stigma about being unemployed than do those who live in areas where unemployment is less common (Hayes and Nutman, 1981). We considered whether contact with other unemployed people reduced the stigma of unemployment and helped to maintain well-being.

In asking respondents about their social interactions with peer groups, we distinguished between those interactions conducted during what might be termed normal working hours (weekdays) and those outside this period (evenings and weekends). Hence respondents were first asked to think about the young people with whom they spent most of their time during the day, from Monday to Friday, and to report whether: all or most were employed; about half were unemployed, half in work; all or most were unemployed. These responses were scored 1, 2 and 3 respectively, with a high score indicating greater contact with other unemployed people. In 1982, when all respondents were unemployed, the proportions responding in each way were 9.2%, 24.1% and 52.8% respectively. Respondents were then asked a similar question, this time referring to the young people with whom they spent their time during evenings or at weekends. In 1982 the proportion reporting that all or most of these contacts were employed was 19.1%, with 36.5% reporting that half were employed and half were unemployed, and 39.4% reporting that all or most were unemployed. These responses were also scored on a scale from 1 to 3.

In 1982, when asked about their weekday contacts, a further 13.7% of the sample reported that they did not spend this time with young people. Four per cent reported this when asked about social contacts during evenings or at weekends. Hence a measure of peer group contact was obtained by giving such respondents a score of 0 and all others a score of 1.

While it seemed plausible that those people with a high proportion of unemployed friends, and those reporting contact with their peer group generally, would be experiencing relatively good psychological health, we also considered whether some types of social contacts during unemployment were associated with poor psychological health. Particularly likely to fall into this category are young people's encounters with others who are perceived as pressing them to obtain a job.

We asked respondents whether they felt under pressure from others to obtain a job. Six items were used to measure the extent of perceived pressure, with each referring to a different source. The items referred to parents, friends, and staff at the Careers Office, Department of Health and Social Security, Unemployment Benefit Office, and Job Centre. Respondents were asked whether they felt under pressure to obtain a job from each of these sources. For each item those responding positively were given a score of 1; all others, including those reporting no contact with the specified source, were given a score of 0. An overall score of perceived pressure was obtained by summing the six items. In 1982 the mean score was 1.20 (s.d. = 1.12).

The associations between these various aspects of respondents' social contacts and their levels of well-being are shown in Table 8.3. Also included is a measure of the stigma respondents reported experiencing from being unemployed. We found that the proportion of unemployed people among the social contacts of those in our 1982 sample was unrelated to their GHQ, depression and anxiety scores. This was true for contacts during weekdays and for those contacts during evenings and weekends. However, those who reported greater contact with other unemployed people tended to report feeling less stigma from being unemployed.

Those people in our sample who reported no contact with others of a similar age during evenings or weekends showed no poorer psychological well-being than those reporting such contact. However, there was a slight tendency for those reporting no contact during weekdays to have higher scores on our well-being measures (indicating poorer mental health) than those reporting such contact.

Table 8.3: Correlations Between Aspects of Social Relationships and Measures of Psychological Well-Being

	GHQ	Depression	Anxiety	Stigma
Unemployed contacts (wd)	-0.02	0.01	-0.04	-0.08**
Unemployed contacts (e/w)	-0.05	-0.06	-0.06	-0.08**
Peer group contact (wd)	-0.06	-0.08**	-0.05	-0.04
Peer group contact (e/w)	-0.01	-0.01	0.00	-0.01
Perceived pressure	0.16***	0.13***	0.14***	0.14***

Note: **p<0.01   ***p<0.001

Finally, we found that those unemployed people in our sample who reported feeling under pressure to get a job from the greatest number of sources also tended to have the highest GHQ, depression and anxiety and stigma scores.

A subsequent stage in our analysis involved assessing the independent contribution to well-being scores of all our measures of supports, contacts and pressures. This was important because some of these variables are likely to have been inter-correlated. To do this we carried out multiple regression analyses, using the well-being variables as outcome measures and the other variables as predictors. Also included among the latter were dummy variables representing the sex and ethnic group of the respondents. This allowed us to control for possible sex and ethnic differences in the level of support, contact and perceived pressure to find a job.

The multiple regression analyses showed that having someone to suggest interesting things to do, and having someone to turn to for help with money, both remained significantly associated with levels of GHQ, depression and anxiety. Other forms of support were found not to be significantly associated with well-being scores.

Perceived pressure to obtain a job retained a significant contribution to the three principal well-being variables, and a higher proportion of unemployed people among the peer group network, both during weekdays and at evenings or weekends, was associated with lower depression scores. However, peer group contact during either of these times, in comparison with no such contact, continued to be unrelated to psychological well-being.

Several important conclusions can be drawn from our findings concerning the social relationships of the unemployed in our sample. First, they show the need for a multi-dimensional concept of social support. Some forms of support were related to the well-being of the unemployed, while others were not. Those which were tended to reflect those areas likely to be of greatest need: money and purposeful activity. Those people who could turn to others for help in both of these ways tended to be coping relatively well, while those people who had no such help tended to be coping relatively poorly. The importance of this kind of instrumental support for unemployed teenagers is consistent with other findings (Schaefer, Coyne and Lazarus, 1981; Parry and Shapiro, 1985), in contrast to earlier work that tended to suggest that emotional support was more important (e.g. Henderson, Byrne, Duncan-Jones, Adcock, Scott and Steele, 1978; Lin, Simeone, Ensel and Kuo, 1979; LaRocco, House and French, 1980). We should note, however, that emotional support, in the form of having someone to turn to for cheering up, was particularly important for female members of our sample.

Second, our results showed that those in our sample reporting contact with other young people, and those spending their time with mainly unemployed people, tended to have lower levels of depression and felt less stigma from being unemployed, respectively. However, these associations were not found to be significant when we used multiple regression analyses to control for other variables. It is possible that these forms of social contact were initially related to well-being because they were associated with the presence of various forms of social support or the lack of perceived pressure.

Finally, we found that perceived pressure to obtain a job was a significant and independent predictor of each of our three well-being measures. Those in our sample reporting being under pressure from the most sources exhibited the highest levels of distress, depression and anxiety. This suggests that it may be important for us not to focus narrowly on the supportive relationships of the unemployed. Although supportive relationships may lessen the burden of unemployment, other relationships may become more strained. Parents, who may have been a source of support when the people in our sample were at school, may have become a source of pressure when they became unemployed. The onset of unemployment may also lead to the establishment of new social contacts which may prove stressful (e.g. with State welfare officials). All of these possibilities point to the need for a broad view to be taken when considering the role of social relationships in helping people to cope with unemployment.

An important point which we have not yet made concerns the correlational nature of the results we have so far reported. Our analyses were cross-sectional and were computed on all those unemployed in 1982. Hence we are unable to specify the causal direction of the associations we observed. While it is possible that the possession of certain forms of support contributed to better psychological well-being, it is equally plausible to suggest that those people with low levels of well-being tended to perceive their social environment as unsupportive. Similarly, poor well-being may cause people to believe that other people are pressurizing them to find a job, rather than such pressure leading to poor well-being. Towards the end of this chapter we describe some longitudinal analyses in which we investigated how far the social supports, contacts and pressures reported by unemployed people in 1983 predicted the changes in their well-being that had occurred since 1982. Such analyses allow us to identify those factors that are associated with an actual decline in well-being. Before that, however, we turn our attention to a third set of variables which may help us to identify good and poor copers among our sample.

3.   ACTIVITIES DURING UNEMPLOYMENT

Several studies point to the importance of leading an active and varied life during unemployment, in so far as this is possible. Those unemployed people who are able to maintain some degree of purposeful activity tend to be more psychologically healthy than those who are less active. Thus Hepworth (1980) reports a study of 78 unemployed men in which a correlation of 0.45 was found between their GHQ score and whether or not their time was fully occupied. Usually, however, the onset of unemployment is associated with an increase in passive behaviours. Warr and Payne (1983), in their sample of 399 unemployed men, found that an increase in behaviours such as sitting around at home, watching television, and listening to the radio, was significantly associated with lower levels of psychological well-being. Similar results have been reported by Warr (1984c) for a sample of 954 unemployed men; this study also showed that an increase in recreational activities, such as hobbies, household repairs and decorating, was associated with lower distress (GHQ) scores. Studies by Fryer and Payne (1984), Feather and Bond (1983) and Haworth and Evans (1987) lend further evidence that purposeful, proactive behaviour during unemployment is beneficial to psychological well-being.

The suggestion that good and poor copers during unemployment may be distinguished by the extent to which they engage in such behaviour is supported by Kilpatrick and Trew (1985). They used time diaries to quantify the daily activities of a sample of 121 unemployed men. Cluster analysis performed on the data revealed four distinct patterns of activity, which the authors labelled Active, Social, Domestic and Passive. Increasingly high GHQ scores were found for these four groups respectively, indicating that poor well-being was associated with decreasing activity and withdrawal into the home.

An explanation of why such activity may protect well-being during unemployment is provided by Jahoda's (1979, 1981, 1982) analysis of the manifest and latent benefits of employment. According to Jahoda, although financial gain is the manifest motivation for being employed, there are also a number of unintended, or latent, benefits which follow from having a job. Employment imposes a time structure on the day, it provides regularly shared experiences and contacts with people outside the immediate family, it provides transcending goals and purposes, a sense of status and identity, and finally it enforces activity. Jahoda suggests that these latent benefits of employment are psychologically supportive and that it is their removal which explains why unemployment is psychologically harmful.

It follows from this that those unemployed people who are able to introduce some of these features into their lives will

134

suffer less psychological damage from not having a job (Henwood and Miles, 1987). Purposeful activity, as well as being itself one of the five latent benefits listed by Jahoda, may also entail the establishment of others. The unemployed person who engages in some sort of time-consuming hobby, for example, may find that this activity also provides him/her with a time structure, achievable goals to work towards, a sense of status or identity, and social contact with others who share the hobby.

We can see, then, that coping behaviour during unemployment may be characterized by this sort of purposeful activity. We investigated how far this was true for the unemployed in our sample by measuring several aspects of their daily activities. We asked unemployed respondents to rate how easy they found it to fill their time, how much time they spent out of the house, the amount of day-to-day variety in their lives, how often they were able to plan their days in advance, and the amount of time they spent with friends. Ratings were on four-point response scales, and were scored such that a high score indicated a more positive response. Correlations between these measures and the three principal well-being measures are shown in Table 8.4.

Our results showed that four of the variables, with the exception of how often respondents were able to plan their days in advance, were significantly negatively correlated with GHQ, depression and anxiety scores. That is, lower scores on these well-being scales were associated with being more able to fill one's time, spending more of one's time out of the house, reporting more day-to-day variety, and spending more time with one's friends. Those unemployed people in our sample who were most active in respect of these variables were therefore among our good copers. In contrast, those who were withdrawing into their homes, being relatively passive, and not sharing much contact with friends, tended to be coping relatively poorly with their experience of unemployment.

Once again this type of cross-sectional analysis cannot identify the causal direction of this relationship. Better psychological well-being may be the outcome of an active and varied life during unemployment, but it may also be a precondition for such a way of life. In all probability the influence is likely to be in both directions. Those unemployed people who are experiencing the least distress or depression may be more inclined to make active use of their spare time, and the ensuing activity is likely to have effects which will maintain or improve their well-being. Longitudinal analyses, to be described below, allowed us to assess how far the level and variety of activity reported in 1983 predicted the degree of change in psychological well-being in the preceding year.

For the moment it is worth noting that the level and variety of activity reported by our unemployed sample does

Table 8.4: Correlations Between Aspects of Daily Activities and Measures of Psychological Well-Being

	GHQ	Depression	Anxiety
Able to fill the time	-0.37	-0.49	-0.29
Time spent out of house	-0.19	-0.17	-0.18
Day-to-day variety	-0.20	-0.20	-0.29
Able to plan days	-0.04	-0.10	-0.02
Time spent with friends	-0.16	-0.15	-0.17

Note: n = 1054, p<0.05 when r = 0.06, p<0.001 when r = 0.09

allow us to distinguish between those with relatively good and those with relatively poor psychological health. Those who were most active may be described as being among our good copers, while those who were the least active were among our poor copers. Moreover, these variables also provide us with a way of explaining some of the sex and ethnic differences in the levels of psychological well-being we observed among our unemployed respondents. In 1982 we found that, generally, males responded more positively to the activity items than did females, and that blacks did so more than did whites. These differences accounted for some, though not all, of the lower levels of well-being found among females and among whites at that time (see Warr, Banks and Ullah, 1985).

4.   INDEPENDENT CONTRIBUTIONS TO WELL-BEING SCORES

So far we have considered how far the level of psychological well-being of unemployed people can be predicted from their scores on certain variables. Three classes of variables have been considered, relating to young people's commitment to finding a job, the supports and pressures they experience from those around them, and their ability to use their spare time constructively, substituting some of the lost benefits of employment. In this section we use multiple regression analyses to identify the contributions to well-being scores made independently by each of the variables. Analyses were computed for whites and blacks separately, and by including a dummy variable representing the sex of the respondent we were also able to see whether the higher GHQ, depression and anxiety scores of unemployed females, when compared with unemployed males, remained after controlling for the effects of the other variables. Amongst unemployed whites in 1983 the simple correlations between sex and GHQ, depression and anxiety were 0.11 ($p<0.01$), 0.10 ($p<0.01$) and 0.18 ($p<0.01$) respectively. Among unemployed blacks the equivalent values were 0.22 ($p<0.001$), 0.18 ($p<0.001$) and 0.19 ($p<0.001$) respectively. In both ethnic groups, higher scores on these well-being variables were associated with females.

Table 8.5 shows the beta weights for all variables in predicting well-being scores among white respondents unemployed in 1983. A measure of financial worries, rated by respondents on a four-point scale, was also included as a predictor variable. A similar table for all unemployed black respondents is shown in Table 8.6.

Among white respondents, sex was no longer significantly associated with GHQ scores, although females continued to have higher depression and anxiety scores. Among black respondents, sex continued to predict significantly scores on all three well-being variables. Thus, although some of the variance in the initially observed sex differences could be

Table 8.5: Beta Coefficients from Multiple Regression Analyses Predicting Psychological Well-Being in 1983 (White Unemployed, n = 641)

	GHQ	Depression	Anxiety
Sex	0.05	0.08*	0.12**
Unemployment duration	0.00	0.01	0.09*
Unemployed contacts (i) weekday	-0.01	-0.01	0.06
(ii) evenings/weekends	0.05	-0.04	0.02
Perceived pressure to get a job	0.11**	0.09*	0.06
Social support:			
Help with money	0.04	0.00	0.01
Someone to talk to	-0.07	-0.06	-0.21**
Interesting things to do	0.02	-0.05	0.07
Cheering up when low	-0.13*	-0.06	-0.10
Information on jobs/benefits	-0.08	-0.10*	-0.01
Financial worries	-0.14***	-0.02	-0.13***
Able to fill the time	-0.18***	-0.31***	-0.12**
Time spent out of house	-0.09*	-0.03	-0.07
Day-to-day variety	0.07	-0.12***	-0.05
Able to plan days	0.05	-0.02	0.03
Time spent with friends	0.06	-0.04	-0.05
Employment commitment	0.06	0.03	0.09
Unemployment orientation	-0.02	-0.07	0.00
Disaffection with youth labour market	0.11**	0.07	0.07
Job search attitude	-0.12*	-0.11*	-0.10
Job expectations	-0.05	0.00	-0.02

Table 8.5 (cont.)

Job applications in last year	-0.01	0.00	0.00
Number of job search methods	0.09*	0.03	0.09
Current job seeking	-0.03	-0.01	-0.10*

Note: * p<0.05, ** p<0.01, *** p<0.001

Table 8.6: Beta Coefficients from Multiple Regression Analyses Predicting Psychological Well-Being in 1983 (Black Unemployed, n = 408)

	GHQ	Depression	Anxiety
Sex	0.19***	0.13***	0.18***
Unemployment duration	-0.11*	0.00	0.02
Unemployed contacts (i) weekday	0.01	-0.02	-0.01
(ii) evenings/weekends	-0.03	0.02	0.01
Perceived pressure to get a job	0.01	0.03	0.09
Social support:			
Help with money	0.02	0.09	0.06
Someone to talk to	0.04	-0.05	-0.09
Interesting things to do	-0.12	-0.08	-0.13*
Cheering up when low	-0.18*	-0.12	-0.13
Information on jobs/benefits	-0.02	-0.12*	0.02
Financial worries	0.08	-0.13**	-0.08
Able to fill the time	-0.16**	-0.24***	-0.10*
Time spent out of house	0.05	-0.03	-0.04
Day-to-day variety	-0.07	-0.14**	0.00
Able to plan days	-0.07	-0.05	-0.02
Time spent with friends	-0.01	-0.02	-0.06
Employment commitment	0.07	0.02	0.13*
Unemployment orientation	0.00	-0.07	0.09
Disaffection with youth labour market	0.07	0.07	0.06
Job search attitude	-0.11	-0.06	-0.10
Job expectations	0.05	-0.03	0.05

Table 8.6 (cont.)

Job applications in last year	0.01	0.11*	0.05
Number of job search methods	0.05	0.07	0.06
Current job seeking	0.01	0.07	-0.09

Note: * p<0.05, ** p<0.01, *** p<0.001

accounted for by the other variables in the equation, by no means could all of it be explained. The poorer psychological well-being of females is therefore likely to be due to factors other than differences between the sexes in terms of level of social support, commitment to finding a job, and use of spare time.

More broadly, the regression equations in Tables 8.5 and 8.6 also identify those variables which, independently, moderate the psychological experience of unemployment. Greater general distress (GHQ) among whites was associated with financial worries, inability to fill the time, disaffection with the youth labour market, perceived pressure to find a job, not having someone to turn to for cheering up, spending less time out of the house, having a more positive job search attitude and using more job search methods. In contrast, general distress among blacks was associated only with shorter periods of the current unemployment spell, absence of help with finding interesting things to do, not having someone to turn to for cheering up, and inability to fill the time.

Depression among whites was associated with perceived pressure to find a job, lack of support with information on jobs and benefits, inability to fill the time, a lack of day-to-day variety, and a more positive job search attitude. Among blacks greater depression was associated with financial worries, inability to fill the time, a lack of day-to-day variety, not having someone to turn to for cheering up or for information on jobs/benefits, and making more job applications.

Anxiety among whites was associated with longer durations of unemployent, not having someone to turn to for help with day-to-day problems, having financial worries, difficulties with filling the time, and less active job-seeking. In contrast, greater anxiety among blacks was associated with not having someone to suggest interesting things to do or to turn to for cheering up, inabililty to fill the time, and high employment commitment.

In conclusion, these analyses identified a number of variables which remained significantly associated with well-being after controlling for other effects. It is also possible to discern a general trend in the pattern of these results. Financial worries were consistently associated with the well-being measures, with those people with the greatest worries experiencing much poorer psychological health. A significant source of the impaired psychological well-being of unemployed people, when compared with their employed counterparts, may therefore lie in the financial worries experienced by the former. Possible reductions in the amount of benefits paid to the unemployed may therefore have the effect of exacerbating the harmful psychological effects already caused by being unemployed.

Other clusters of variables which distinguished between those coping relatively well and those coping relatively poorly with unemployment are those concerned with the amount of social support received from others, the level of activity of the unemployed person, and their commitment, both attitudinal and behavioural, to finding a job. Those people coping the least well were those who lacked the support of those around them, those who were the least active and who led relatively routine lives, and those who most strongly desired a job and were making the most effort to find one. In counselling the young unemployed, therefore, it may be important to encourage contact with others who are in a position to help, the adoption of activities which are likely to structure a person's day and get them out of the house, and a focussing of job-seeking activity rather than wasteful and depressing efforts being expended pursuing avenues which are likely to be unproductive.

5.   VARIABLES ASSOCIATED WITH CHANGES IN PSYCHOLOGICAL WELL-BEING

So far we.have examined the associations of several groups of variables with the levels of psychological well-being found among our unemployed respondents. In this way we have been able to identify those features which characterise those people who are coping relatively well with being unemployed, and those people who are not coping so well. However, such an approach portrays a rather static view of coping behaviour, since it is based on associations which are found at one single point in time. In order to capture the likely dynamic aspects of these coping strategies we used longitudinal analyses. In particular we examined the changes in psychological well-being that had occurred amongst those continuously unemployed from 1982 to 1983. In this way we were able to identify those who were learning to cope with their unemployment, and who showed an improvement in their levels of well-being. We could also identify those who were failing to cope and whose well-being was deteriorating as they continued to remain unemployed. In this section we see whether any of the variables we have so far considered, relating to job-seeking, social support, and daily activities, were associated with improvements or deteriorations in the psychological well-being of these young people.

Changes in well-being scores were computed by subtracting the 1982 score from the 1983 score. A change score with a positive value therefore indicates a higher GHQ, depression or anxiety score in 1983 than in 1982 and hence a deterioration in psychological well-being. A change score with a negative value indicates an improvement in well-being. Multiple regression analyses were used to identify those variables,

143

measured in 1983, which significantly predicted changes in well-being. Examination of the intercept values for each regression equation revealed that a positive association between the predictor variable and a change score indicated that a higher level of the predictor variable was associated with a greater deterioration in well-being. Likewise, a negative association indicated that a higher score on the predictor variable was associated with less deterioration in well-being. In these analyses scores on the well-being variables in 1982 were included as co-variates in the prediction of change between interviews, thus controlling for differences in the levels of well-being found in 1982. The beta coefficients and significance levels are shown in Table 8.7.

An increase in general psychological distress (GHQ) was associated with an inability to fill the time, not having someone to turn to for cheering up, disaffection with the youth labour market, and perceived pressure from others to find a job. Increases in depression were also associated with more social pressure to find a job and an inability to fill the time, as well as a lack of day-to-day variety and not having someone to turn to for information on jobs and benefits. Finally, increases in anxiety were significantly associated with greater perceived pressure to get a job, being less able to fill the time, not having someone to turn to for help with money, and with females.

6. CONCLUSION

In this chapter we have used various kinds of analyses to identify the variables that are associated with levels of psychological well-being during unemployment. By doing this we have been able to characterise those people who tended to be coping relatively well with their unemployment, and those who tended to be coping relatively poorly. Some of these variables represent actions which are largely under the control of the unemployed, such as their job-seeking activities. Others refer to features of the environment of the unemployed person, such as supportive or pressurizing friends and family. The kind of help which might be given to unemployed people, in order to lessen the psychological harm caused by unemployment, should therefore be a combination of advice to the unemployed themselves, recommending those actions which tend to be associated with good psychological well-being, and efforts to change or maintain certain features of their environment, which can include the attitudes of others as well as things like benefit levels.

Our choice of variables has been guided by theories about the possible causes of psychological distress during unemployment. Three classes of variables were examined, relating to job-seeking, social supports and pressures, and activities. Each were found to be associated with levels of well-being among our unemployed sample, providing important empirical evidence in support of these theories.

Cross-sectional analyses showed that poorer psychological well-being tends to be associated with greater efforts being made to find a job. This is consistent with the frustrated work motivation pattern suggested by Feather, and suggests that a significant source of psychological ill-health during unemployment lies in failed attempts to secure a job. Our results fail to support a "learned helplessness" model of depression, which predicts that greater depression will be associated with lower levels of job-seeking as the unemployed person "learns" that he or she is likely to fail at most tasks. However, among white respondents, those reporting lower levels of job seeking activity tended to have higher levels of anxiety. It is possible that "scaling down" job-seeking efforts may protect the unemployed from the depression caused by failure but may at the same time lead to greater anxiety about the future due to the decreased likelihood of getting a job.

Various kinds of social support were found to be associated with higher levels of psychological well-being amongst our unemployed respondents. In 1983 , those people who possessed the emotional support of someone whom they could turn to for cheering up had lower distress scores than those who lacked this support, this being true for blacks and whites, males and females. In 1982, having someone to turn to for financial support and someone to suggest interesting things to do were both significantly associated with lower GHQ, depression and anxiety scores.

Longitudinal analyses identified those people who did not have someone to provide information on jobs and/or benefits as being more likely to have experienced an increase in their level of depression. The lack of a consistent pattern in these relationships suggests that the role of social support in lessening the harmful psychological effects of unemployment is somewhat complex. Only certain forms of support appear to be beneficial, and then only at certain points in time. The type of support which is associated with better psychological well-being may therefore reflect the current needs of the unemployed person, needs which are likely to change as their spell of unemployment continues.

Those people reporting a higher proportion of unemployed people among their social contacts tended to report feeling less stigma from being unemployed. However, this association was not statistically significant after controlling for other forms of support. The proportion of unemployed contacts, and that of the amount of contact with other young people, were both unrelated to our principal well-being measures. However, perceived pressure from others to get a job was consistently

Table 8.7: Beta Coefficients from Multiple Regression Analyses Predicting Changes in Psychological Well-Being

	GHQ	Depression	Anxiety
1982 well-being score	-0.62***	-0.68***	-0.61***
Sex	0.04	0.01	0.11
Ethnic group	-0.03	-0.03	-0.03
Unemployment duration	-0.01	0.04	-0.03
Unemployed contacts (i) weekdays	0.04	-0.01	0.05
(ii) evenings/weekends	0.01	0.02	0.05
Perceived pressure to get a job	0.11*	0.10*	0.13**
Social support:			
Help with money	0.04	0.00	0.09
Someone to talk to	0.00	0.02	-0.12
Interesting things to do	0.10	0.00	-0.03
Cheering up when low	-0.15	-0.09	-0.04
Information on jobs/benefits	-0.08	-0.12*	-0.04
Financial worries	-0.06	-0.01	-0.08
Able to fill the time	-0.20***	-0.36***	-0.17*
Time spent out of house	-0.03	-0.01	-0.07
Day-to-day variety	-0.06	-0.15**	-0.04
Able to plan days	0.08	0.00	0.06
Time spent with friends	-0.09	-0.05	-0.09
Employment commitment	0.00	0.03	-0.03
Unemployment orientation	-0.04	-0.03	-0.05
Disaffection with youth labour market	0.16*	0.06	0.08

Table 8.7 (cont.)

Job search attitude	0.01	0.06	0.08
Job expectations	-0.07	-0.04	-0.03
Job applications in last year	0.01	-0.01	0.01
Number of job search methods	0.01	-0.06	-0.02
Current job seeking	0.04	0.04	0.01

Note: * p<0.05, ** p<0.01, *** p<0.001

associated with poorer well-being, and with an actual deterioration in well-being over the course of the two interviews. Although on the whole we found that our respondents were reporting feeling under pressure from fewer sources in 1983 than in 1982, these results still point to the importance of sympathy and understanding from those who are in contact with the young unemployed.

The third class of variables included in our analyses related to the quality and level of the activities of our unemployed respondents. Overall associations were found between our three measures of psychological well-being and the degree to which these people were able to fill their time during the day, the amount of time they spent out of the house and with their friends, and the amount of variety in their day-to-day lives. These features may be seen as corresponding to some of the latent benefits of employment listed by Jahoda (1981). In particular, they are likely to be associated with a time structure for the day, shared experiences and contacts with people outside the immediate family, goals and purposes, and degree of activity. Moreover, we are also able to characterise the unemployed person who experiences poor psychological well-being as someone who sits at home most of the time, going through the same routines each day and who has long periods of inactivity. Such a characterisation is similar to the "passive" life-style observed among unemployed men by Kilpatrick and Trew (1985) and who had particularly high GHQ scores.

Of the variables considered in this class, ability to fill the time and the amount of day-to-day variety maintained a significant contribution to well-being scores after controlling for other variables. Longitudinal analyses showed they were also related to changes in well-being from 1982 to 1983, with those reporting being most able to fill their time and those living the most varied lives experiencing the least deterioration in their psychological well-being.

While our analyses point to the importance of substituting some of the latent benefits of employment, they also point to the importance of the manifest benefit of having a job - that of receiving pay. Greater financial worries among the unemployed in our sample were significantly associated with higher GHQ and anxiety scores among whites and with higher depression scores among blacks. These associations were independent of any of the activity variables. The greater financial hardship of unemployment, therefore, may serve to impair a person's psychological well-being irrespective of how much effort they are putting into leading an active and varied life without a job.

Finally, our analyses have allowed us to interpret some of the meaning of the sex and ethnic differences in levels of well-being found in our sample (Warr, Banks and Ullah, 1985; Banks and Ullah, 1986). Sex and ethnicity are most usefully

148

viewed as proxies for other variables, indicating social and psychological differences between the broad categories of male and female, black and white. Thus if whites have higher distress scores than blacks it is pertinent to consider the other ethnic differences of which this may be a reflection. The pattern of results we obtained over the course of the whole study suggests that the poorer well-being of whites, compared with blacks, in 1982 was partly due to their greater commitment to finding a job. There was also evidence at that time that blacks were reporting higher activity levels than were whites. Thus we have reported that after controlling for these variables, black males did not have significantly higher GHQ scores than white males (Warr, Banks and Ullah, 1985). However, ethnic differences in GHQ scores were still observed among females, while ethnic differences in depression were found among both males and females. Clearly, then, other factors were contributing to these differences in well-being.

A similar interpretation can be made in terms of the differences in well-being observed between males and females. In 1982 some of this difference could be accounted for by the higher levels of employment commitment and lower levels of activity found among females than among males (Warr, Banks and Ullah, 1985). In 1983, after controlling for these and other variables, white females were found not to have significantly higher GHQ scores than white males (see Table 8.5). However, differences in depression and anxiety scores remained, and were present on all three well-being measures among black respondents. Among females, then, there are likely to be other factors, not measured here, which are contributing to their relatively poor well-being scores during unemployment.

Chapter 9

CONCLUDING COMMENTS

Without restating our findings in any great detail we now wish
to make a few concluding remarks about the context of this
research, and about some broader issues concerned with youth
unemployment.

Some commentators are now saying that youth unemployment
has disappeared, mainly as a result of the rapid expansion of
the Youth Training Scheme. Most certainly, for many 16 and 17
year olds the current predominant route is from school to YTS
and into a job, an extended but successful transition. But
for others their destination is still unemployment, whether
straight after school leaving or via YTS. Some slip through
the net of youth training immediately whilst for others
unemployment is merely delayed. More importantly, however, in
this research we are talking about a cohort for whom
unemployment was a very real experience, and who will carry
the scars of that experience with them all their lives (cf.
Fineman, 1987). It seems to us to be wrong to diminish their
lives by arguing that youth unemployment has largely 'gone
away'.

1.   WELL-BEING AND ATTACHMENT TO THE LABOUR MARKET

What are our general conclusions about the well being and
labour market attachment of this sample of unemployed youth?
In this study we have looked at the well-being of young people
with varying lengths of unemployment, up to a maximum of two
and a half years after leaving school. Despite exhaustive
statistical analysis, we found no association between
unemployment duration and general psychological distress,
depression or anxiety. The only statistical test to reach
even moderate significance was on males, amongst whom the
greatest distress was found in the shortest and in the longest
duration categories (thus suggesting a curvilinear
relationship). Thus, with a large sample, the results confirm
earlier findings (e.g. Feather and Davenport, 1981; Warr,

150

Jackson and Banks, 1982; Finlay-Jones and Eckhardt, 1984), that for the 16-18 year age group length of unemployment and psychological well-being are not directly and simply related. Furthermore, neither was there any psychological deterioration, as assessed by longitudinal measures, between the first and second years in the labour market. This finding is all the more surprising since analyses controlled for whether or not individuals were continuously unemployed, for sex and ethnicity.

It seems from this finding, therefore, that some form of adjustment to unemployment has been made, even though, as in previous studies (Banks et al., 1980; Banks and Jackson, 1982; McPherson and Hall, 1983) the young unemployed report significantly more psychological distress than their employed counterparts. But one important caveat must be added. The well-being inventories used here typically call for a comparison of recent feelings with those felt in the past few years, with the response categories typically being "more so than usual", "same as usual", "less so than usual", and "much less so than usual". It is our belief that in responding to these types of questions people are really reporting recent changes, and not comparing the present with several years ago. Thus, chronic states of depression or anxiety will to some extent be missed by such inventories. This deficiency has been recognized in the literature only rarely (e.g. Goodchild and Duncan-Jones, 1985).

Given the consistently large differences in psychological distress between the unemployed and the employed, the question arises of whether it is the experience of unemployment itself that accounts for the differences. Earlier research focussed on controlling for differences prior to entering the labour market, whilst the young people were still at school (e.g. Banks and Jackson, 1982; Patton and Noller, 1984; Feather and O'Brien, 1986a). The conclusion from these studies is that the experience of unemployment is more likely to create psychological distress, rather than the converse. Another way of looking at this issue of causality is to see if changes in status are accompanied by expected psychological changes. So for those moving from employment to unemployment an increase in distress would be expected, whilst for those moving from unemployment to employment a decline in distress would be expected. An earlier study of a smaller sample found this to be so, but called for replication on larger samples (Jackson et al., 1983). The present study clearly identifies the beneficial and reversible effects associated with moving into employment.

The increased risk of 'GHQ caseness' (those scoring over the threshold score) was a factor of 2.7 for the unemployed compared to the employed. This increased risk applied equally to males and females. The percentages falling into this category were 29.9 of unemployed males, 40.9 of unemployed females, 11.2 of employed males and 15 of employed females. Furthermore, there was convincing evidence that psychological symptoms occurred after the start of unemployment, and roughly half were attributed by the young people to unemployment. Whilst we find this evidence convincing in demonstrating the destructive element to unemployment, we note that not all research is in agreement with our conclusions (Feather and O'Brien, 1986b).

The second major theme to our research has been concerned with what might be called attachment to the labour market, conceived of in both attitudinal and behavioural terms. One clear message emerging was that young people still want to be gainfully employed, and not just for financial reasons. Furthermore, there was hardly any evidence of acceptance or enjoyment of the unemployment experience. The significant change over time was an increasing sense of discouragement, reflected in a fall-off in job-seeking and related activities. By analysing in depth the characteristics of those who had become seriously detached from the labour market we conclude that there is a real danger of the emergence of ghettoes of chronically unemployed and disaffected young people, who will find it increasingly difficult to integrate themselves with the institutions of employment.

Guided by theories about the possible causes of psychological distress during unemployment three major classes of variables were examined, to help us understand what was happening in the lives of these young people. These are focussed on job seeking, social supports and pressures, and activities. Each of these groups, to differing extents, determined which individuals coped better or worse with unemployment, and the implications of these findings for various theoretical positions have been spelled out in Chapter 8.

2.   ETHNIC AND SEX DIFFERENCES

We have referred already to the research literature on employment discrimination, and a balanced summary is provided by the Report from the Select Committee of the House of Lords (1982). All ethnic minorities constitute around one million workers (including the unemployed) out of a total workforce of around 26 million. During the 1980s the ethnic minority population as a whole has grown faster than the rest of the population, especially so in the cities. In general, ethnic minorities are to be found in a few low paid, unskilled or semi-skilled occupations, requiring little training and offering poor prospects. The evidence indicates that this disadvantaged position in the labour market cannot be attributable to lack of educational qualifications.

The special vulnerability of black school-leavers has been highlighted in the Commission for Racial Equality Lewisham study which found that the increased risk of unemployment compared to white school-leavers was a factor of three (CRE, 1978). Other evidence submitted to the Scarman Report indicated that 55% of black males under 19 in Brixton were registered as unemployed in 1981 (The Scarman Report, 1981). The main factors underlying the greater vulnerability of black people at times of high and rising unemployment are: a) their over-representation in occupations most at risk, b) language and cultural disadvantages in finding new jobs, and c) employment discrimination. From research carried out in Birmingham at the end of the 1970s it is known that young blacks in search of skill training through apprenticeships find themselves in a disadvantaged position (Lee and Wrench, 1981). It was argued that this arises from two factors: minority youth knowledge and awareness of how the labour market operates, and the approach of employers to recruitment and selection of skilled workers. The result is a particularly powerful form of indirect discrimination. From the MSC's survey of YTS leavers between April 1985 and January 1986 it was shown that the chances of finding employment after YTS were lower for young people living in areas of high unemployment, for those with no educational qualifications, and for young black people. Furthermore, young blacks are less likely to get a place on employer-led YTS schemes that offer a better chance of finding employment afterwards. And amongst those blacks who do get on the better schemes post-YTS employment rates are lower than amongst their white counterparts.

In our own study blacks were similarly disadvantaged in their future job prospects. But importantly, this disadvantage was shown to be present after controlling for differences in educational qualification, level of job seeking activity, and the unemployment rate of the area in which they lived. But the question of whether ethnicity influences the psychological response to unemployment has rarely been addressed, prior to the present project.

In general, the topic of epidemiological research into health differences between ethnic groups is beset by many methodological difficulties (e.g. Rack, 1982). Evidence that does exist suggests that rates of minor psychological disturbance among blacks born in Britain are similar to those among British-born whites (Cochrane, 1979). In the present study, at first interview in 1982 the unemployed white 17 year olds (both male and female) exhibited significantly higher distress (GHQ) and depression than their black counterparts (detailed in Warr, Banks and Ullah, 1985). By the time of the second interviews the differences had disappeared. We are reasonably confident that the earlier differences can be accounted for by the initially greater commitment to finding a job amongst the whites. By 1983 this commitment had fallen and levelled off at the same strength as that of the blacks. In addition, there was evidence of higher activity levels among blacks in 1982, a factor known to be associated with better mental health (see, for example, Warr, 1987). It seems highly unlikely that ethnicity (or more correctly, skin colour) by itself is a useful explanatory variable in this context. What seem more important are the attitudinal and behavioural variables which are 'carried' by the ethnic group variable. Another finding of note was that amongst blacks very few of the factors examined in this project were useful in predicting who would and who wouldn't deteriorate more, in a psychological sense, as a result of continued unemployment. Indeed, the only significant factor was an inability to fill the time, which predicted an increase in depression.

Taken as a whole, therefore, with the notable exception of the relationship between changing aspirations and well-being during unemployment, there are not very many important differences between the ethnic groups. Whilst of course ethnic identity differences are crucial in understanding the socialisation of youth it appears from this research that the fundamental orientations to the labour market and responses to unemployment are similar for blacks and whites, with the exception of the previously mentioned time sequence of reduced aspiration.

Recently some writers (e.g. Griffin, 1985b) have criticised the research literature on unemployment as being male-dominated. Whether or not this has been the case in the past, the criticism now is harder to sustain. As demonstrated in earlier chapters, there are sometimes complex differences between the sexes in the way they respond to unemployment, as well as some similarities. Whilst for males the predominant career aim after leaving school is still to secure the wage, the situation has not changed to the extent that females can be regarded in exactly the same way. Undoubtedly, increasingly larger numbers of young women expect to spend most of their adult life in employment, interrupted by short spells of child-bearing and child-rearing. But at the same time it is also clear from our research that some young women still actively disengage from the labour market, via parenthood, as an alternative to battling against adverse labour market conditions. For young people of both sexes with the same goals and aspirations, however, the consequences of unemployment are not going to be all that dissimilar. Neither sex copes particularly better than the other with the distressing nature of extended joblessness.

3. POLITICAL INVOLVEMENT OF THE YOUNG UNEMPLOYED

It has often been something of a surprise to discover how the unemployed do not become mobilized as a political force (e.g. Marsh, Fraser and Jobling, 1985), especially since the causes of and proposed solutions to unemployment are portrayed in the media as being largely political. Schlozman and Verba (1979) suggest that on the whole the unemployed are not drawn into political movements because they are offered no ideologies linking their personal predicament to collective action. The unemployed see it as someone else's responsibility to do something about the problem as a whole, whilst seeking personal solutions themselves. The strongest motivation is to escape from the pool of unemployed, not to proclaim membership of it. The research literature on the politics of the unemployed is scant when compared to the unemployment literature as a whole. Three studies that specifically focussed on unemployed youth are those of Clark (1985), Gaskell and Smith (1985) and Breakwell (1986), from which it can be concluded that there is considerable disenchantment with or apathy towards the mainstream political system and that the young unemployed express clear verbal attitudes in favour of direct political action, lawbreaking and violent change. However, to what extent these attitudes are translated into real action is less clear (Jackson, 1985). These previously cited studies suffer somewhat from small sample sizes and from interviewing individuals who had not experienced extensive unemployment. In our own unemployed cohort we were able to ask a few political questions at the second interview, shortly after the 1983 General Election. Details of the questions and the results are available elsewhere (Banks and Ullah, 1987), so only the conclusions will be given. When compared with the employed, the unemployed were more disaffected with the political system, more likely to support the Labour Party, less likely to support the Conservative Party, more likely to have voted Labour in the 1983 General Election and less likely to have voted Conservative. Ethnic comparisons indicated that blacks were more politically disaffected than whites (cf. Gaskell and Smith, 1984), were more likely than whites to express support for the Labour Party, and were more likely to vote Labour in the General Election. The only major sex difference was amongst whites, such that males were more likely to support the National Front, and females more likely to support Labour. These results, then, tend to confirm some of the previous findings and are interpreted as indicating increased detachment from the main political system for some unemployed young people, and with increased attachment to Labour politics among others.

Whilst there is considerable agreement, therefore, on the lack of political involvement of the young unemployed,

155

research to date can be criticised for having focussed on only a narrowly defined band of conventional party political questions. Clearly the study of political socialisation should encompass much broader dimensions such as attitudes to and representations of trade unions, government, law and order, citizenship, sexual politics and so forth. It will not be long before the new ESRC 16-19 Initiative begins to make important contributions to this area of research (Bynner, 1987).

4. CIVIL UNREST AND CRIME

There are those who would try to blame all the evils of modern society on unemployment (and often by implication, the Government). And specifically in respect of youth unemployment three of those evils are soccer hooliganism, urban riots, and crime. Although these are found to be concentrated largely in our big cities, where unemployment rates are the highest, correlations do not imply causation and in some cases they can be plainly misleading since a third factor can be associated with both phenomena. In this case the third factor is almost certainly the nature of life in the modern inner city. Political philosophers have long predicted that very large cities would produce masses of "hooligans and barbarians"; that something in the alienated and anonymous urban way of life was guaranteed to bring out anti-social tendencies. In historical analysis the uprooting of citizens from rural areas to live and work in cities has been linked to change, usually of a negative kind, in the traditional religious, moral and political values. Equally, we are now living through an age of radical economic restructuring during which the traditional work demands and disciplines of heavy manufacturing industry are disappearing. From the backcloth of unemployment there is no escaping, but to blame soccer hooliganism simply on unemployment or on poverty is untenable. From all accounts most soccer hooligans are certainly not poor, and if they are unemployed they show great resourcefulness in raising funds to travel to matches, pay entrance fees and pay for the large amounts of drink consumed. Indeed, some of the most vicious thuggery associated with soccer matches is perpetrated by a particularly affluent species - the 'casual' or equivalent regional variation, of which each city or club has its own brand. The attendant and trivial style wars have been documented (e.g. Redhead and McLaughlin, 1985) in a fascinating way, but it has little to do with unemployment other than providing a forum for the acting out of insensitive and cruel prejudices. Redhead and McLaughlin describe how Liverpool and Everton fans are goaded about the poverty of Merseyside when they visit London. It is claimed that London casuals flashed £5 and £10 notes in the same manner as the Metropolitan Police did on the Yorkshire coalfield during the miners' strike. The same authors quote other insults aimed at fans from economically run-down areas:

> Sign on, sign on with hope in your heart,
> And you'll never get a job

and,

> One job between you,
> You've only got one job between you.

Here, then, it seems that unemployment, and especially the regional disadvantage associated with it, provides just another piece of bait in the tribal hatred that many young people regard as quite normal. To explain soccer violence in terms of social problems does not seem a profitable activity. Instead effort should be concentrated on controlling it.

The anatomy of street riots is a somewhat different matter, although, as in the case of soccer hooliganism, the action is staged against a backcloth of inner city social and environmental decay. The Scarman Report on the 1981 Brixton riots documents two views on the cause of the riots:

(i) The first was that they were caused by oppressive policing over a period of years, and especially by the harassment of young blacks on the streets of Brixton. According to this view the few hundred young people at the centre of the riot were "anti-police", and the explanation stopped there.

(ii) The second view was that the riots "were a protest against society by people, deeply frustrated and deprived, who saw in a violent attack upon the forces of law and order their one opportunity of compelling public attention to their grievances".
(The Scarman Report, 1981, p.2)

Scarman goes on to stress that both views tend to over-simplify what is a complex situation, in which the policing problem cannot be understood except in the context of a multi-racial community in a deprived inner city area where unemployment, especially among young black people, is high and hopes are low.

The disturbances that afflicted other major cities, such as St. Pauls in Bristol, Toxteth in Liverpool and Handsworth in Birmingham, perhaps did not attract the same depth of analysis. Nonetheless, from the available evidence the previously mentioned social and economic problems are common to all whilst the spark that ignited the fire varied according to locality. Most commentators now acknowledge the complexity

157

and seriousness of the problem, which calls for economic and environmental regeneration of the inner cities combined with a strong and sensitive law and order policy.

At the individual level some of the immediate personal consequences of unemployment, in particular having to fill day after day with some kind of goal-directed activity and having to eke out state benefits to meet the basic requirements of life, create the kinds of pressures and opportunities for crime to flourish. To test out this hypothesis in individuals, however, must rank as one of the most difficult and challenging research questions. As mentioned in Chapter 3 the consensus in the literature, identified by Freeman and Medoff (1982), is that crime may be an alternative for youth without paid work. The House of Lords Select Committee on Unemployment (1982) also conclude tentatively that from anecdotal evidence, supported by some factual data, there is a causal link. The Committee report evidence from ad hoc surveys of the status of detected offenders, from correlations between crime and unemployment rates across time and areas, and from comparisons between unemployment and changes in the prison population. Whilst interpretations of this kind of data are hedged with uncertainty because of changes in sentencing policy, factors influencing detection rates and so on, nonetheless the evidence is pretty convincing. What is also of interest are the longer term consequences for those young unemployed who drift into casual delinquency and crime, and in doing so cut themselves off from a return to normal, legal, employment opportunities. Longitudinal information on such at risk groups does not exist at present, but it would be valuable to see research carried out on the lagged effects of high youth unemployment levels.

5. FINAL REMARKS

In the next few years demographic changes, resulting from a falling birthrate, together with policy initiatives will to some extent relieve pressure on the youth labour market. But our sample of 1981's school leavers, now into their twenties, contain many young people who are largely unqualified, untrained and living in economically depressed parts of the country. As things stand they may be considered to have little to look forward to. Despite a growing isolation from the world of work, these people were found to be still keen to be employed, not unrealistic in their wage demands and generally inward looking in terms of the effect unemployment was having upon them. Other recent studies, such as that of Coffield et al. (1986) which uses quite different methodologies, tend to be pointing in the same direction.

Finally, Beveridge was probably not the first to observe how "misery generates hate", and other Western countries understood long ago that the worst possible start in adult life was from the back of the dole queue. Initiatives such as the Community Programme and the Job Training Scheme for over 18 year olds may not come too soon as the belated first rung on the ladder. There was once a time when the transition from school to work was largely non-problematic, with frequent job-changing being the only identified problem. But as we have argued throughout this book, the situation has changed radically and is still in a state of flux. Now extended and varied transitions are the norm. As a research topic the study of the social and psychological consequences of early careers is experiencing a long overdue growth spurt. We hope that in relation to a particular type of early career taken by some of the more disadvantaged youth we have contributed to the broader understanding of one of the most serious social problems of the 1980s.

Adams, A.V. and Mangum, G.L. (1978) The Lingering Crisis of Youth Unemployment, W.E. Upjohn Institute: Kalamazoo, MI

Aries, P. (1962) Centuries of Childhood, Jonathan Cape, London

Ashton, D.N. and Field, D. (1976) Young Workers: From School to Work, Hutchinson, London

Ashton, D.N. and Maguire, M.J. (1986) Young Adults in the Labour Market, Department of Employment Research Paper No. 55, London

Ashton, D.N., Maguire, M.J. and Garland, V. (1982) Youth in the Labour Market, Department of Employment Research Paper No. 34, London

Bachman, J.G., O'Malley, P.M. and Johnston, J. (1978) Youth Transition, Volume VI: Adolescence to Adulthood - Change and Stability in the Lives of Young Men, Institute for Social Research: Ann Arbor, MI

Banks, M.H. (1983) 'Validation of the General Health Questionnaire in a Young Community Sample', Psychological Medicine, 13, 349-353

Banks, M.H., Clegg, C.W., Jackson, P.R., Kemp, N.J., Stafford, E.M. and Wall, T.D. (1980) 'The Use of the General Health Questionnaire as an Indicator of Mental Health in Occupational Studies', Journal of Occupational Psychology, 53, 187-194

Banks, M.H. and Jackson, P.R. (1982) 'Unemployment and Risk of Minor Psychiatric Disorder in Young People: Cross-Sectional and Longitudinal Evidence', Psychological Medicine, 12, 789-798

Banks, M.H., Mullings, C. and Jackson, E.J. (1983) 'A Bench-Mark for Youth Opportunities', Employment Gazette, 91 (3), 91-95

Banks, M.H. and Ullah, P. (1986) 'Unemployment and Less Qualified Urban Youth', Employment Gazette, 94, 205-210

Banks, M.H. and Ullah, P. (1987) 'Political Attitudes and Voting Among Unemployed and Employed Youth', Journal of Adolescence, 10, 201-206

Barber, A. (1985) 'Ethnic Origin and Economic Status', Employment Gazette, 93 (12), 467-477

Baxter, J.L. (1975) 'The Chronic Job-Changer: A Study of Youth Unemployment', Social and Economic Administration, 9 (3), 184-206

Beales, A.L. and Lambert, R.S. (1934) Memoirs of the Unemployed, Gollancz, London

Becker, O.E. and Hills, S.M. (1981) 'Youth Attitudes and Adult Labour Market Activity', Industrial Relations, 20 (1), 60-70

Berg, I. (1973) Education and Jobs, Penguin, Harmondsworth

Beveridge, W.H. (1909) Unemployment: A Problem of Industry, Longmans, Green and Co., London (reprinted in 1930)

Beveridge, W.H. (1944) Full Employment in a Free Society, George Allen and Unwin, London

Blood, M.R. (1969) 'Work Values and Job Satisfaction', Journal of Applied Psychology, 53 (6), 456-459

Bosanquet, N. and Doeringer, P.B. (1973) 'Is there a Dual Labour Market in Great Britain?', Economic Journal, 83, 421-435

Branthwaite, A. and Garcia, S. (1985) 'Depression in the Young Unemployed and Those on Youth Opportunities Schemes', British Journal of Medical Psychology, 58, 67-74

Breakwell, G.M. (1986) 'Political and Attributional Responses of the Young, Short-Term Unemployed', Political Psychology, 7, 265-278

Breakwell, G.M., Harrison, B. and Propper, C. (1984) 'Explaining the Psychological Effects of Unemployment for Young People: The Importance of Specific Situational Factors', British Journal of Guidance and Counselling, 12 (2), 132-140

Breen, S. (1984) 'Status Attainment or Job Attainment?', British Journal of Sociology, 35 (3), 363-386

Brenner, M.H. (1971) 'Economic Changes and Heart Disease Mortality', American Journal of Public Health, 61, 606-611

Brenner, M.H. (1973) Mental Illness and the Economy, Harvard University Press: Cambridge, MA

Brenner, M.H. (1979) 'Mortality and the National Economy: A Review, and the Experience of England and Wales', The Lancet, 2, 568-573

Brenner, M.H. (1980a) 'Industrialization and Economic Growth: Estimates of their Effects on the Health of Populations' in M.H. Brenner, A. Mooney and T.J. Nagy (eds.), Assessing the Contributions of the Social Sciences to Health, American Academy for the Advancement of Science, Washington

Brenner, M.H. (1980b) 'Importance of the Economy to the Nation's Health' in L. Eisenberg and A. Kleinman (eds.), The Relevance of Social Science for Medicine, Reidel, New York

Brenner, M.H. and Mooney, A. (1982) 'Economic Change and Sex-Specific Cardiovascular Mortality in Britain 1955-1976', Social Science and Medicine, 16, 431-442

Brown, G. and Harris, T. (1978) Social Origins of Depression: A Study of Psychiatric Disorder in Women, Tavistock, London

Bynner, J. (1987) 'Coping with Transition: ESRC's New 16-19 Initiative', Youth and Policy, in press

Cameron, C., Lush, A. and Meara, G. (1943) Disinherited Youth: A Report on the 18+ Age Group, T. and A. Constable, Edinburgh

Caplan, G. (1974) Support Systems and Community Mental Health, Behavioral Publications, New York

Carter, M.P. (1969) Into Work, Penguin, Harmondsworth

Cassel, J.C. (1976) 'The Contribution of the Social Environment to Host Resistance', American Journal of Epidemiology, 104, 107-123

Catalano, R., Dooley, C.D. and Jackson, R. (1981) 'Economic Predictors of Admissions to Mental Health Facilities in a Non-Metropolitan Community', Journal of Health and Social Behaviour, 22, 284-297

Cherry, N. (1976) 'Persistent Job Changing - Is It a Problem?', Journal of Occupational Psychology, 49, 203-221

Clark, A.W. (1985) 'The Effects of Unemployment on Political Attitude', Australian and New Zealand Journal of Sociology, 21 (1), 100-108

Clarke, L. (1980a) The Transition from School to Work: A Critical Review of Research in the United Kingdom, HMSO, London

Clarke, L. (1980b) Occupational Choice: A Critical Review of Research in the United Kingdom, HMSO, London

Clough, E., Gray, J. and Jones, B. (1987) 'Those Who Say 'No' to YTS: Findings from the National Youth Cohort Survey', British Journal of Education and Work, in press

Cobb, S. (1976) 'Social Support as a Moderator of Life Stress', Psychosomatic Medicine, 38, 300-314

Cochrane, R. (1979) 'Psychological and Behavioural Disturbance in West Indians, Indians and Pakistanis in Britain: A Comparison of Rates Among Children and Adults', British Journal of Psychiatry, 134, 201-210

Coffield, F., Borrill, C. and Marshall, S. (1983) 'How Young People Try to Survive Being Unemployed', New Society, 64, 1072, 332-334

Coffield, F., Borrill, C. and Marshall, S. (1986) Growing Up at the Margins, Open University Press, Milton Keynes

Commission for Racial Equality (1978) Looking for Work: Black and White School Leavers in Lewisham, HMSO, London

Cook, D.G., Cummins, R.O., Bartley, M.J. and Shaper, A.G. (1982) 'Health of Unemployed Middle-Aged Men in Great Britain', The Lancet, June 5, 1290-1294

Cook, J.D., Hepworth, S.J., Wall, T.D. and Warr, P.B. (1981) The Experience of Work: A Compendium and Review of 249 Measures and their Use, Academic Press, London

Cook, T.D. and Campbell, D.T. (1976) 'The Design and Conduct of Quasi-Experiments and True Experiments in Field Settings' in M.D. Dunnette (ed.), Handbook of Industrial and Organizational Psychology, Rand McNally, Chicago

Daily Mirror (1982) Letter in 7th May edition

Daniel, W.W. (1974) A National Survey of the Unemployed, Political and Economic Planning, London

Daniel, W.W. and Stilgoe, E. (1977) 'Where are they Now?', Political and Economic Planning, No. 572, London

Deacon, A. (1978) 'The Scrounging Controversy: Public Attitudes Towards the Unemployed in Contemporary Britain', Social and Economic Administration, 12, 120-135

Dex, S. (1979) 'A Note on Discrimination in Employment and its Effects on Black Youths', Journal of Social Policy, 9, 357-369

Dex, S. (1982) 'Black and White School Leavers: The First Five Years of Work', Department of Employment Research Paper No. 33

Dex, S. (1983) 'Recurrent Unemployment in Young Black and White Males', Industrial Relations Journal, 14 (1), 41-49

Doeringer, P.B. and Piore, M.J. (1971) Internal Labour Markets and Manpower Analysis, D.C. Heath and Company: Lexington, MA

Donovan, A. and Oddy, M. (1982) 'Psychological Aspects of Unemployment: An Investigation into the Emotional and Social Adjustment of School-Leavers', Journal of Adolescence, 5, 15-30

Dore, R. (1976) The Diploma Disease, Allen and Unwin, London

Eisenberg, P. and Lazarsfeld, P.F. (1938) 'The Psychological Effects of Unemployment', Psychological Bulletin, 35, 358-390

Erikson, E.H. (1968) Identity: Youth and Crisis, Faber, London

Eysenck, H.J. (1953) The Structure of Human Personality, John Wiley, New York

Feather, N.T. (1982) 'Unemployment and its Psychological Correlates: A Study of Depressive Symptoms, Self-Esteem, Protestant Ethic Values, Attributional Style, and Apathy', Australian Journal of Psychology, 34 (3), 309-323

Feather, N.T. and Barber, J.G. (1983) 'Depressive Reactions and Unemployment', Journal of Abnormal Psychology, 92 (2), 185-195

Feather, N.T. and Bond, M.J. (1983) 'Time Structure and Purposeful Activity Among Employed and Unemployed University Graduates', Journal of Occupational Psychology, 56, 241-254

163

Feather, N.T. and Davenport, P.R. (1981) 'Unemployment and Depressive Affect: A Motivational and Attributional Analysis', Journal of Personality and Social Psychology, 41 (3), 422-436

Feather, N.T. and O'Brien, G.E. (1986a) 'A Longitudinal Study of the Effects of Employment and Unemployment on School-Leavers', Journal of Occupational Psychology, 59, 121-144

Feather, N.T. and O'Brien, G.E. (1986b) 'A Longitudinal Analysis of the Effects of Different Patterns of Employment and Unemployment on School-Leavers', British Journal of Psychology, 77, 459-479

Ferguson, T. and Cunnison, J. (1951) The Young Wage Earner: A Study of Glasgow Boys, Oxford University Press, London

Fineman, S. (1987) 'Back to Unemployment: Wounds and Wisdoms' in D. Fryer and P. Ullah (eds.), Unemployed People: Social and Psychological Perspectives, Open University Press, Milton Keynes

Finlay-Jones, R. and Eckhardt, B. (1981) 'Psychiatric Disorder Among the Young Unemployed', Australian and New Zealand Journal of Psychiatry, 15, 265-270

Finlay-Jones, R. and Eckhardt, B. (1984) 'A Social and Psychiatric Survey of Unemployment Among Young People', Australian and New Zealand Journal of Psychiatry, 18, 135-143

Flaim, P.O. (1973) 'Discouraged Workers and Changes in Unemployment', Monthly Labour Review, 96 (3), 8-16

Freeman, A. (1914) Boy Life and Labour: The Manufacture of Inefficiency, P.S. King and Son, London

Freeman, R.B. and Medoff, J.L. (1982) 'The Youth Labor Market Problem in the United States: An Overview' in R.B. Freeman and D.A. Wise (eds.), The Youth Labour Market Problem: Its Nature, Causes and Consequences, University of Chicago Press, Chicago

Fryer, D. and Payne, R. (1984) 'Proactive Behaviour in Unemployment: Findings and Implications', Leisure Studies, 3, 273-295

Fryer, D. and Payne, R. (1986) 'Being Unemployed: A Review of the Literature on the Psychological Experience of Unemployment' in C.L. Cooper and I. Robertson (eds.), International Review of Industrial and Organizational Psychology, John Wiley, Chichester

Furnham, A. (1982) 'The Protestant Work Ethic and Attitudes Towards Unemployment', ournal of Occupational Psychology, 55, 277-285

Furnham, A. (1983) 'Mental Health and Unemployment Status: A Preliminary Study', British Journal of Guidance and Counselling, 11 (2), 197-201

Furnham, A. (1984) 'Unemployment, Attribution Theory, and Mental Health: A Review of the British Literature', International Journal of Mental Health, 13 (1/2), 51-67

Gaskell, G. and Smith, P. (1981) '"Alienated" Black Youth: An Investigation of "Conventional Wisdom" Explanations', New Community, 9 (2), 182-193

Gaskell, G. and Smith, P. (1985) 'An Investigation of Youth's Attributions for Unemployment and their Political Attitudes', Journal of Economic Psychology, 6, 65-80

Gillis, J.R. (1974) Youth and History, Academic Press, New York

Ginzberg, E., Ginsberg, S.W., Axelrad, S. and Herma, J.L. (1951) Occupational Choice, Columbia University Press, New York

Goldberg, D. (1972) The Detection of Psychiatric Illness by Questionnaire, Oxford University Press, London

Goldberg, D. (1978) anual of the General Health Questionnaire, NFER Publishing Company, Windsor

Goldberg, D. (1981) 'Estimating the Prevalence of Psychiatric Disorder from the Results of a Screening Test' in J.K. Wing, P. Bebbington and L.N. Robins (eds.), What is a Case?, Grant McIntyre, London

Goodchild, M.E. and Duncan-Jones, P. (1985) 'Chronicity and the General Health Questionnaire', British Journal of Psychiatry, 146, 55-61

Gordon, D.M. (1972) Theories of Poverty and Underemployment, Lexington Books: Lexington, MA

Gore, S. (1978) 'The Effect of Social Support in Moderating the Health Consequences of Unemployment', Journal of Health and Social Behaviour, 19, 157-165

Gough, H.G. (1957) Manual for the California Psychological Inventory, Consulting Psychologists Press: Palo Alto, CA

Grainger, R. (1980) Unemployment and Crime: A Critique of Methodology, Solicitor General of Canada, Ottawa

Griffin, C. (1985a) 'Whatever Happened to Mandy?', New Society, 2nd May, 152-154

Griffin, C. (1985b) Typical Girls, Routledge and Kegal Paul, London

Gurney, R.M. (1980a) 'The Effects of Unemployment on the Psycho-Social Development of School-Leavers', Journal of Occupational Psychology, 53, 205-213

Gurney, R.M. (1980b) 'Does Unemployment Affect the Self-Esteem of School Leavers?', Australian Journal of Psychology, 32, 3, 175-182

Gurney, R.M. (1981) 'Leaving School, Facing Unemployment, and Making Attributions about the Causes of Unemployment', Journal of Vocational Behaviour, 18, 79-91

Halford, W.K. and Learner, E. (1984) 'Correlates of Coping with Unemployment in Young Australians', Australian Psychologist, 19 (3), 333-344

Harris, M. (1960) 15-18: Report of the Central Advisory Council for Education, Vol. II (Surveys), HMSO, London

Harrison, R. (1976) 'The Demoralising Experience of Prolonged Unemployment', Department of Employment Gazette, 84, 339-348

Haworth, J.T. and Evans, S.T. (1987) 'Meaningful Activity and Unemployment' in D. Fryer and P. Ullah (eds.), Unemployed People: Social and Psychological Perspectives, Open University Press, Milton Keynes

Hayes, J. and Nutman, P. (1981) Understanding the Unemployed, Tavistock, London

Henderson, S.K., Byrne, D.G., Duncan-Jones, P., Adcock, S., Scott, R. and Steele, G.P. (1978) 'Social Bonds in the Epidemiology of Nurses: A Preliminary Communication', British Journal of Psychiatry, 132, 463-466

Henderson, S.K., Duncan-Jones, P., Byrne, D.G., Scott, R. and Adcock, S. (1979) 'Psychiatric Disorder in Canberra', Acta Psychiatrica Scandinavica, 60, 355-374

Hendry, L.B., Raymond, M. and Stewart, C. (1984) 'Unemployment, School and Leisure: An Adolescent Study', Leisure Studies, 3, 175-187

Henwood, F. and Miles, I. (1987) 'The Experience of Unemployment and the Sexual Division of Labour' in D. Fryer and P. Ullah (eds.), Unemployed People: Social and Psychological Perspectives, Open University Press, Milton Keynes

Hepworth, S. (1980) 'Moderating Factors of the Psychological Impact of Unemployment', Journal of Occupational Psychology, 53, 139-146

Hesketh, B. and Shouksmith, G. (1982) 'Reasons Given for Being Unemployed and the Job Search Process', New Zealand Journal of Industrial Relations, 7, 137-144

Hill, J. (1978) 'The Psychological Impact of Unemployment', New Society, 43, 118-120

Hirsch, D. (1983) Youth Unemployment: A Background Paper, Youthaid, London

House of Lords (1982) Report from the Select Committee of the House of Lords on Unemployment, Volume I - Report, HMSO, London

Jackson, M.P. (1985) Youth Unemployment, Croom Helm, London

Jackson, P.R., Stafford, E.M., Banks, M.H. and Warr, P.B. (1983) 'Unemployment and Psychological Distress in Young People: The Moderating Role of Employment Commitment', Journal of Applied Psychology, 68 (3), 525-535

Jackson, P.R. and Warr, P.B. (1984) 'Unemployment and Psychological Ill-Health: The Moderating Role of Duration and Age', Psychological Medicine, 14, 605-614

Jahoda, M. (1979) 'The Impact of Unemployment in the 1930s and the 1970s', Bulletin of the British Psychological Society, 32, 309-314

Jahoda, M. (1981) 'Work, Employment and Unemployment: Values, Theories and Approaches in Social Research', American Psychologist, 36, 184-191

Jahoda, M. (1982) _Employment and Unemployment_, Cambridge University Press, Cambridge

Jenkins, R. (1983) _Lads, Citizens and Ordinary Kids: Working-Class Youth Lifestyles in Belfast_, Routledge and Kegan Paul, London

Jewkes, J. and Jewkes, S. (1934) _The Juvenile Labour Market_, Gollancz, London

Jewkes, J. and Winterbottom, A. (1933) _Juvenile Unemployment_, Allen and Unwin, London

Jones, B., Gray, J. and Clough, E. (1987) 'Finding a Post-16 Route - The First Year's Experience' in R. Coles (ed.), _The Search for Jobs and the New Vocationalism_, Gower, Aldershot

Kasl, S.V. (1982) 'Strategies of Research on Economic Instability and Health', _Psychological Medicine_, 12, 637-649

Kasl, S.V. and Cobb, S. (1980) 'The Experience of Losing a Job: Some Effects on Cardiovascular Functioning', _Psychotherapy and Psychosomatics_, 34, 88-109

Kasl, S.V., Gore, S. and Cobb, S. (1975) 'The Experience of Losing a Job: Reported Changes in Health, Symptoms and Illness Behaviour', _Psychosomatic Medicine_, 37, 106-122

Kaufman, H.G. (1982) _Professionals in Search of Work: Coping with the Stress of Job Loss and Underemployment_, John Wiley, New York

Keil, E.T., Riddell, D.S. and Green, B.S.R. (1966) 'Youth and Work: Problems and Perspectives', _Sociological Review_, 14 (2), 117-137

Kelvin, P. and Jarrett, J.E. (1985) _Unemployment: Its Social and Psychological Effects_, Cambridge University Press, Cambridge

Kett, J.F. (1977) _Rites of Passage_, Basic Books, New York

Kidd, J.M. and Knasel, E.G. (1980) _Work Values and Work Salience: A Review of British and North American Research_, NICEC, Hatfield

Kilpatrick, R. and Trew, K. (1985) 'Lifestyles and Psychological Well-Being Among Unemployed Men in Northern Ireland', _Journal of Occupational Psychology_, 58, 207-216

Kosky, R. (1980) 'Unemployment and the Mental Health of Adolescents', _Australian Family Physician_, 9, 845-848

Langner, T.A. (1962) '22-Item Screening Scores of Psychiatric Symptoms Indicating Impairment', _Journal of Health and Social Behaviour_, 1, 267-276

LaRocco, J.M., House, J.S. and French, J.R.P. (1980) 'Social Support, Occupational Stress, and Health', _Journal of Health and Social Behaviour_, 21, 202-218

Lee, G. and Wrench, J. (1981) _In Search of a Skill: Ethnic Minority Youth and Apprenticeships_, Commission for Racial Equality, London

Lee, G. and Wrench, J. (1984) 'Routes into Segmented Youth Labour Markets', International Journal of Social Economics, 11 (7), 77-90

Liem, R. and Rayman, P. (1984) 'Perspectives on Unemployment, Mental Health and Social Policy', International Journal of Mental Health, 13 (1/2), 3-17

Lin, N., Simeone, R.S., Ensel, W.M. and Kuo, W. (1979) 'Social Support, Stressful Life Events, and Illness: A Model and Empirical Test', Journal of Health and Social Behaviour, 20, 108-119

Maizels, J. (1970) Adolescent Needs and the Transition from School to Work, Athlone Press, London

Makeham, P. (1980) 'The Anatomy of Youth Unemployment', Employment Gazette, 88 (3), 235-236

Manpower Services Commission (1978) Young People and Work, Manpower Services Commission, London

Manpower Services Commission (1981a) A New Training Initiative: An Agenda for Action, HMSO, London

Manpower Services Commission (1981b) Review of Services for the Unemployed, HMSO, London

Marks, C. (1981) 'Split Labour Markets and Black-White Relations, 1865-1920', Phylan, XLII (4), 293-308

Marsden, D. and Duff, E. (1975) Workless, Pelican, Harmondsworth

Marsh, C., Fraser, C. and Jobling, R. (1985) 'Political Responses to Unemployment' in B. Roberts, R. Finnegan and D. Gallie (eds.), New Approaches to Economic Life: Economic Restructuring, Unemployment and the Social Division of Labour, Manchester University Press, Manchester

Marsh, D.C. (1965) The Changing Social Structure of England and Wales, 1871-1961, Routledge and Kegan Paul, London

Martin, J. and Roberts, C. (1984) Women and Employment: A Lifetime Perspective, HMSO, London

McIntosh, M. (1979) 'The Welfare State and the Needs of the Dependent Family' in S. Burman (ed.), Fit Work for Women, Croom Helm, London

McPherson, A. and Hall, W. (1983) 'Psychiatric Impairment, Physical Health and Work Values Among Unemployed and Apprenticed Young Men', Australian and New Zealand Journal of Psychiatry, 11, 335-340

Millham, S., Bullock, R. and Hosie, K. (1978) 'Juvenile Unemployment: A Concept Due for Re-cycling?', Journal of Adolescence, 1, 11-24

Mirels, H. and Garrett, J. (1971) 'The Protestant Ethic as a Personality Variable', Journal of Consulting and Clinical Psychology, 36, 40-44

Nicholson, N. (1984) 'A Theory of Work-Role Transitions', Administrative Science Quarterly, 27, 172-191

Bibliography

O'Brien, G.E. and Kabanoff, B. (1979) 'Comparison of Unemployed and Employed Workers on Work Values, Locus of Control and Health Variables', Australian Psychologist, 14, 143-154

Oddy, M., Donovan, A. and Pardoe, R. (1984) 'Do Government Training Schemes for Unemployed School Leavers Achieve Their Objectives?: A Psychological Perspective', Journal of Adolescence, 7, 377-385

O'Malley, P.M. and Bachman, J.G. (1979) 'Self-Esteem and Education: Sex and Cohort Effects Among High School Seniors', Journal of Personality and Social Psychology, 37, 1153-1159

Osterman, P. (1981) 'Interpreting Youth Unemployment', New Society, 27th August, 344-346

Parry, G. and Shapiro, D.A. (1985) 'Social Support and Life Events in Working Class Women: Stress Buffering or Independent Effects?', Archives of General Psychiatry, 43, 315-323

Patton, W. and Noller, P. (1984) 'Unemployment and Youth: A Longitudinal Study', Australian Journal of Psychology, 36 (3), 399-413

Payne, R., Warr, P.B. and Hartley, J. (1984) 'Social Class and Psychological Ill-Health During Unemployment', Sociology of Health and Illness, 6, 152-174

Phillips, D. (1973) 'Young and Unemployed in a Northern City' in D. Weir (ed.), Men and Work in Modern Britain, Fontana London

Platt, S. (1984) 'Unemployment and Suicidal Behaviour: A Review of the Literature', Social Science and Medicine, 19, 93-115

Platt, S. and Kreitman, N. (1985) 'Unemployment and Parasuicide Among Men in Edinburgh 1968-1982', Psychological Medicine, 15, 113-123

Rack, P. (1982) Culture, Race and Mental Disorder, Tavistock, London

Raffe, D. (1983) 'Employment Instability Among Less Qualified Young Workers', British Journal of Guidance and Counselling, 11 (1), 21-34

Raffe, D. (1984) 'Youth Unemployment and the MSC: 1977-1983' in D. McCrone (ed.), Scottish Government Yearbook, Unit for the Study of Government in Scotland, University of Edinburgh

Redhead, S. and McLaughlin, E. (1985) 'Soccer's Style Wars', New Society, 16 August, 225-228

Roberts, K. (1971) From School to Work, David and Charles, Newton Abbot

Roberts, K., Duggan, J. and Noble, M. (1981) Unregistered Youth Unemployment and Outreach Careers Work: Part One, Non-Registration, Department of Employment Research Paper No. 31, London

Roberts, K., Duggan, J. and Noble, M. (1983) 'Racial Disadvantage in Youth Labour Markets' in L. Barton and S. Walker (eds.), Race, Class and Education, Croom Helm, London

Roberts, K., Noble, M. and Duggan, J. (1982a) Unregistered Youth Unemployment and Outreach Careers Work: Part Two, Outreach Careers Work, Department of Employment Research Paper No. 32, London

Roberts, K., Noble, M. and Duggan, J. (1982b) 'Youth Unemployment: An Old Problem or a New Lifestyle?', Leisure Studies, 1, 171-182

Roberts, K. Noble, M. and Duggan, J. (1984) 'Youth Unemployment: An Old Problem or a New Lifestyle?' in K. Thompson (ed.), Work, Employment and Unemployment, Open University Press, Milton Keynes

Rosenberg, M. (1965) Society and the Adolescent Self-Image, Princeton University Press: Princeton, NJ

Rosier, M.J. (1978) Early School Leavers in Australia, IEA Monograph Studies No. 7, Almquist and Wiksell, Stockholm

Rowntree, B.S. and Lasker, B. (1911) Unemployment: A Social Study, Macmillan, London

Rutter, M. (1979) Changing Youth in a Changing Society, The Nuffield Provincial Hospitals Trust, London

Schaefer, C., Coyne, J.C. and Lazarus, R.S. (1981) 'The Health-Related Functions of Social Support', Journal of Behavioral Medicine, 4, 381-405

Schlozman, K.L. and Verba, S. (1979) Injury to Insult: Unemployment, Class and Political Response, Cambridge University Press, Cambridge

Shepherd, D.M. and Barraclough, B.M. (1980) 'Work and Suicide: an Empirical Investigation', British Journal of Psychiatry, 136, 469-478

Smith, D.J. (1976) The Facts of Racial Disadvantage, Political and Economic Planning, Vol. XLIII, No. 560

Smith, D.J. (1981) Unemployment and Racial Minorities, Policy Studies Institute, No. 594

Snaith, R.P., Bridge, W.K. and Hamilton, M. (1976) 'The Leeds Scale for the Self-Assessment of Anxiety and Depression', British Journal of Psychiatry, 128, 156-165

Stafford, E.M. (1982) 'The Impact of the Youth Opportunities Programme on Young People's Employment Prospects and Psychological Well-Being', British Journal of Guidance and Counselling, 10 (1), 12-21

Stafford, E.M., Jackson, P.R. and Banks, M.H. (1980) 'Employment, Work Involvement and Mental Health in Less Qualified Young People', Journal of Occupational Psychology, 53 291-304

Stokes, G. and Cochrane, R. (1984) 'The Relationship Between National Levels of Unemployment and the Rate of Admission to Mental Hospitals in England and Wales, 1950-1976', Social Psychiatry, 19, 117-125

Bibliography

Super, D.E. (1957) The Psychology of Careers, Harper and Row, New York

Tawney, R.H. (1909) 'Economics of Boy-Labour', Economic Journal, 19, 517-537

The Pilgrim Trust (1938) Men Without Work, Cambridge University Press, Cambridge

The Scarman Report (1981) The Brixton Disorders 10-12 April 1981: Report of an Inquiry by the Rt. Hon. The Lord Scarman, OBE, Cmnd. 8427, HMSO, London

The Sunday Times (1983) Feature article in 21st August edition

Thoits, P.A. (1982) 'Conceptual, Methodological, and Theoretical Problems in Studying Social Support as a Buffer Against Stress', Journal of Health and Social Behaviour, 23, 145-159

Thomas, D. (1985) 'Taking the Measure of Unemployment', New Society, 16 May, 223-225

Tiggemann, M. and Winefield, A.H. (1980) 'Some Psychological Effects of Unemployment in School Leavers', Australian Journal of Social Issues, 15 (4), 269-276

Tiggemann, M. and Winefield, A.H. (1984) 'The Effects of Unemployment on the Mood, Self-Esteem, Locus of Control and Depressive Affect of School Leavers', Journal of Occupational Psychology, 57, 33-42

Townsend, P. (1979) Poverty in the United Kingdom, Penguin, Harmondsworth

Turtle, A.M., Cranfield, D., Rogers, D.H., Reuman, B. and Williams, J. (1978) 'Life - Hot In It: A Psychological Comparison of Employed and Unemployed Sydney Youth', Vocational Guidance Research Bulletin, 4, 73-81

Turtle, A.M. and Ridley, A. (1984) 'Is Unemployment a Health Hazard? Health-Related Behaviours of a Sample of Unemployed Sydney Youth in 1980', Australian Journal of Social Issues, 19 (1), 27-42

Ullah, P. (1985) 'Disaffected Black and White Youth: The Role of Unemployment Duration and Perceived Job Discrimination', Ethnic and Racial Studies, 8, 181-193

Ullah, P. (1987) 'Unemployed Black Youths in a Northern City' in D. Fryer and P. Ullah (eds.), Unemployed People: Social and Psychological Perspectives, Open University Press, Milton Keynes

Ullah, P. and Banks, M.H. (1985) 'Youth Unemployment and Labour Market Withdrawal', Journal of Economic Psychology, 6, 51-64

Ullah, P., Banks, M.H. and Warr, P.B. (1985) 'Social Support, Social Pressures and Psychological Distress During Unemployment', Psychological Medicine, 15, 283-295

Verbrugge, L.M. (1983) 'Multiple Roles and Physical Health of Women and Men', Journal of Health and Social Behavior, 24, 16-30

171

Warr, P.B. (1982) 'A National Study of Non-Financial Employment Commitment', <u>Journal of Occupational Psychology</u>, <u>55</u>, 297-312

Warr, P.B. (1984a) 'Job Loss, Unemployment and Psychological Well-Being' in V. Allen and E. van de Vliert (eds.), <u>Role Transitions</u>, Plenum Press, New York

Warr, P.B. (1984b) 'Work and Unemployment' in P.J.D. Drenth, H. Thierry, P.J. Willems and C.J. de Wolff (eds.), <u>Handbook of Work and Organisation Psychology</u>, John Wiley, London

Warr, P.B. (1984c) 'Reported Behaviour Changes After Job Loss', <u>British Journal of Social Psychology</u>, <u>23</u>, 271-275

Warr, P.B. (1985) 'Twelve Questions About Unemployment and Health' in B. Roberts, R. Finnegan and D. Gallie (eds.), <u>New Approaches to Economic Life</u>, Manchester University Press, Manchester

Warr, P.B. (1987) <u>Work, Unemployment and Mental Health</u>, Oxford University Press, London

Warr, P.B., Banks, M.H. and Ullah, P. (1985) 'The Experience of Unemployment Among Black and White Urban Teenagers', <u>British Journal of Psychology</u>, <u>76</u>, 75-87

Warr, P.B. and Jackson, P.R. (1983) 'Self-Esteem and Unemployment Among Young Workers', <u>Le Travail Humain</u>, <u>46</u>, 355-366

Warr, P.B. and Jackson, P.R. (1985) 'Factors Influencing the Psychological Impact of Prolonged Unemployment and of Re-employment', <u>Psychological Medicine</u>, <u>15</u>, 795-807

Warr, P.B., Jackson, P.R. and Banks, M.H. (1982) 'Duration of Unemployment and Psychological Well-Being in Young Men and Women', <u>Current Psychological Research</u>, <u>2</u>, 207-214

Warr, P.B. and Parry, G. (1982) 'Depressed Mood in Working-Class Mothers With and Without Paid Employment', <u>Social Psychiatry</u>, <u>17</u>, 161-165

Warr, P.B. and Payne, R. (1983) 'Affective Outcomes of Paid Employment in a Random Sample of British Workers', <u>Journal of Occupational Behaviour</u>, 4, 91-104

Weber, M. (1904) <u>The Protestant Ethic and the Spirit of Capitalism</u>, Allen and Unwin, London

West, M. and Newton, P. (1983) <u>The Transition from School to Work</u>, Croom Helm, London

White, M. (1983) <u>Long-Term Unemployment and Labour Markets</u>, Policy Studies Institute, No. 622

Wilder, C.S. (1980) <u>Selected Health Characteristics by Occupation, United States 1975-6</u>, US Department of Health and Human Services, Hyattsville, Maryland

Willis, P. (1977) <u>Learning to Labour: How Working Class Kids Get Working Class Jobs</u>, Saxon House, London

Winefield, A.H. and Tiggemann, M. (1985) 'Psychological Correlates of Employment and Unemployment: Effects, Predisposing Factors, and Sex Differences', <u>Journal of Occupational Psychology</u>, <u>58</u>, 229-242

Bibliography

Zung, W.W.K. (1965) 'A Self-Rating Depression Scale', <u>Archives of General Psychiatry</u>, <u>12</u>, 63-70

Zung, W.W.K (1974) 'The Measurement of Affects: Depression and Anxiety' in P. Pichot and R. Olivier-Martin (eds.), <u>Psychological Measurements in Psychopharmacology</u>, S. Karger, Basel

Author Index

SUBJECT INDEX

Subject Index

social
    class 16-7, 35
    contact 21, 100, 126-33
    pressure 23, 126-33, 145
    support 20-1, 23, 126-33
special measures 9-10, 13, 24
stage theory 57, 80-1
status attainment model 17
stigma 20, 59, 60, 64, 66,
    129, 145
suicide 19

time structure 100, 103
training 9-11, 13-5, 23
transition from school to
    work 6-7, 13

unemployment
    and age 32
    and ethnicity 35-8
    and health 19
    and sex differences 34-8
    and school leavers 22
    and social activities 21
    at risk groups 3-6
    attitudes towards 9, 72-9
    duration 23, 36, 51, 54,
        59-62, 86, 105
    in the Great Depression
        3-5
    mediating factors in
        response to 7, 16,
        19-20, 121-49

vocational
    choice 34
    training 11, 13

withdrawal from the labour
    market 18, 23, 84, 99-109
work ethic - see Protestant
    Work Ethic
Work Experience Programme 13
work
    salience 73
    values 73
workshy stereotype 73-4

Youth Cohort Study 15, 47
youth labour market
    changes 8-15
    structure 18-9, 22, 32
    theories of 12-3
Youth Opportunities Programme
    10, 13-4, 36, 39, 52, 53
    54
Youth Training Scheme 10,
    14-5, 150
youth unemployment
    at risk groups 3, 8
    causes 3
    rates 3, 8-10, 14
    trends 8-15

Zung Anxiety Scale 58, 60
    62-5
Zung Depression Scale 53, 55,
    58, 60, 62-5

180